The Urban Girl's Manifesto

Melody Biringer

CRAVE Vancouver: The Urban Girl's Manifesto

A publication of The CRAVE Company
1805 12th Ave W #A
Seattle WA 98119
206.282.0173

thecravecompany.com/vancouver
twitter.com/cravevancouver
facebook.com/cravevancouver

While every effort was made to ensure the accuracy of the information, details are subject to change so please call ahead. Neither The CRAVE Company nor CRAVE Vancouver shall be responsible for any consequences arising from the publication or use. All editorial content in this publication is the sole opinion of CRAVE Vancouver and our contributing writers.

Printed in the United States of America

ISBN 978-0-9847143-9-1
Fourth Edition
January 2013
$19.95 CAD

The Urban Girl's Manifesto

We CRAVE Community.
We believe in acknowledging, celebrating and passionately supporting local businesses. CRAVE is a celebration of women entrepreneurs that showcases creative, interesting and gutsy proprietors. By introducing you to the savvy businesswomen in this guide, we hope that we will help inspire your own inner entrepreneur.

We CRAVE Adventure.
We encourage you to break your routine, to venture away from your regular haunts, to visit new businesses, to explore all the funky finds and surprising spots that Vancouver has to offer. Whether it's to hunt for a birthday gift, indulge in a spa treatment or connect with like-minded people, let CRAVE Vancouver be your guide for a one-of-a-kind hometown adventure.

We CRAVE Quality.
CRAVE is all about quality products and thoughtful service. We know that a satisfying shopping trip requires more than a simple exchange of money for goods, and that a rejuvenating spa date entails more than a quick clip of the cuticles and a swipe of polish. We know you want to come away feeling uplifted, beautiful, excited, relaxed, relieved and, above all, knowing you got the most bang for your buck. We have scoured the city to find the hidden gems, new hot spots and old standbys, all with one thing in common: they're the best of the best!

A Guide to Our Guide

CRAVE Vancouver is more than a guidebook. It's a savvy, quality-of-lifestyle book devoted entirely to local businesses owned by women. CRAVE Vancouver will direct you to some of the best local spots—top boutiques, spas, cafés, stylists, fitness studios and more. And we'll introduce you to the inspired, dedicated women behind these exceptional enterprises, for whom creativity, quality, innovation and customer service are paramount.

Not only is CRAVE Vancouver an intelligent guide for those wanting to know what's happening throughout town, it's a directory for those who value the contributions that spirited businesswomen make to our region.

Photos by Vairdy Photography, except portrait by Malcolm Parry

Della Optique
Optometry & Eyewear

Kitsilano, Vancouver

Expert. Personal. Delightful.
Remaining at the forefront of the latest eyewear and sunglass trends for more than 10 years, Della Optique's discerning staff provide expert assistance in selection from an extensive collection of unique designer frames and sunglasses. You can conveniently have your eyes examined by the eye doctor and get contact lenses, glasses and sunglasses all in the same location—complete eye care!

Dr. Della Chow

Q&A

What do you like best about owning a business?
The flexibility and freedom to take care of my clients the way I want. Creating a beautiful store and positive environment for my staff and myself. Happy, appreciative clients.

Who is your role model or mentor?
My mentor is my own optometrist who is now retired. I grew up in a small town, Prince George. He treated everyone well and was passionate about his profession.

What motivates you on a daily basis?
How hard my parents worked in our Chinese restaurant. When the restaurant closed after 40 years, the local newspaper wrote about how much they would miss it.

Specialties: Eye Exams, Designer Frames and Sunglasses
2589 W Broadway, Vancouver
604.742.3937, dellaoptique.com

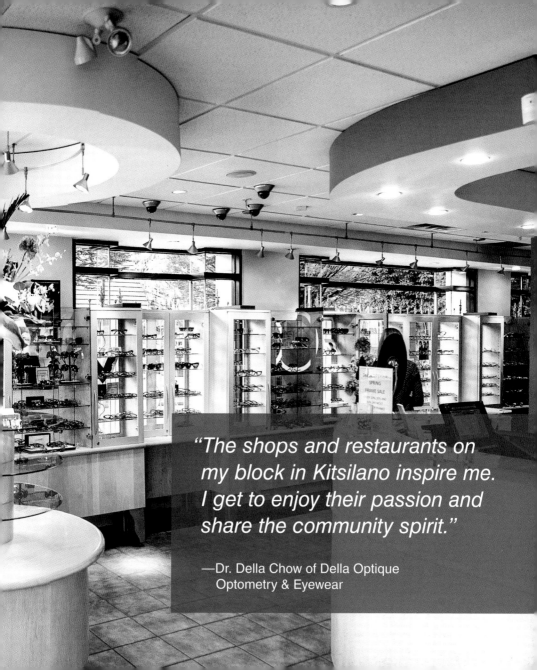

"The shops and restaurants on my block in Kitsilano inspire me. I get to enjoy their passion and share the community spirit."

—Dr. Della Chow of Della Optique
   Optometry & Eyewear

Q&A

What tip would you give women who are starting a business?
Just go for it. The whole process is unreal, and the challenge of it will change your perception of yourself in a positive way. Believe in yourself, and know that you can do so much more than you ever even realized.

What do you like best about owning a business?
The creativity. The space that you create can be an expression of your mood and, even at a deeper level, your soul.

Who is your role model or mentor?
My sister. She set the bar extremely high in my family. It is because of her that there has never been a doubt in my mind that I can create whatever kind of life I want for myself.

Suka Yee

Acupoint Wellness Centre

Downtown Vancouver

Compassionate. Holistic. Peaceful.

A boutique wellness centre in downtown Vancouver, providing alternative health services that help restore well-being, balance and relaxation in a compassionate and healing environment. Specializing in acupuncture, biopuncture, vitamin and homeopathic injections, and massage therapy.

Specialties: Biopuncture, Massage Therapy, and Acupuncture
981 Hornby St, Vancouver, 604.688.7710
acupoint.ca
facebook.com/acupointwellnesscentre

Photos by Jennifer Williams

Carolyn Williams

Q&A

What tip would you give women
who are starting a business?
Running a business can be daunting
and lonely, so having other women
to talk with who have shared similar
experiences can be a real life saver.

Who is your role model or mentor?
My mom has been my role model since
the day I was born, but what was truly
remarkable was watching her beat
cancer and come out even healthier
on the other side. Between The Bar
Method and yoga, she is still taking
five to six exercise classes a week!

What motivates you on a daily basis?
Seeing our clients work so hard
in class pushes me to create the
best possible environment and
workout for them that I can.

The Bar Method

Yaletown and West Vancouver

Personal. Intense. Rewarding.

The Bar Method is a one-hour core-strengthening exercise program, combining yoga, Pilates and ballet to lengthen, strengthen and sculpt the body. The Bar Method provides a targeted workout, which includes fat-burning interval training, muscle-shaping isometrics, ballet conditioning and physical therapy to quickly sculpt the entire physique. Muscles look longer and more defined, and the body becomes leaner and more slender.

Specialty: The Bar Method Classes
837 Beatty St, Ste 201, Vancouver, 604.681.6188
vancouver.barmethod.com, Twitter: @BarMethod_Van
facebook.com/BarMethodVancouver
1760 Marine Dr, Ste 250, West Vancouver, 604.925.6199
west-vancouver.barmethod.com
facebook.com/pages/The-Bar-Method-West-Vancouver

the bar

"My motto is 'Onwards and upwards.' I constantly remind myself to learn from the past while at the same time continue to move forward."

—Carolyn Williams of The Bar Method

Baobei Lashes & Company

Vancouver, British Columbia

Unique. Luxe. Elegant.
Baobei Lashes brings the ultimate creme de la creme lashes to market—flexible for easy application. Made of 100 percent mink fur, these strip lashes can be used up to 25 times with proper care and won't harm the environment like regular plastic lashes that are used only a handful of times before needing to be tossed. They are uber lightweight and flexible for easy application and you won't be fighting the corners from peeling up at the end of the night. Feel how naturally full your lash line will be.

Specialty: Mink Fur False Lashes
888.406.5274, baobeilashes.com
Twitter: @baobei_lashes

Photos by Kari Heese

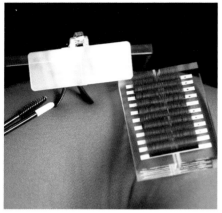

Judy Anderson

Q&A

What tip would you give women who are starting a business?
Follow your heart, be realistic about what you are capable of doing and do it perfectly.

What do you like best about owning a business?
Being able to manage my own schedule so that I can fit in quality time with those that I love. God willing, it will be a family of my own one day... Until then, it's all about my staff, clients, friends and my mom.

What motivates you on a daily basis?
Competition. It never ceases to amaze me how many young, vibrant entrepreneurial minds are working hard every second of the day. It really keeps you going.

{SUNDAY}

{MONDAY}

"*Success is a great thing, but the whole point is to achieve success so that you can enjoy the little things! If you lose sight of that, you've missed the target.*"

—Judy Anderson of Baobei
    Lashes & Company

Because You Said So...

Vancouver, British Columbia

Organized. Creative. Driven.
Because You Said So... (BYSS...) is a unique promotions and events company that combines 30 years of experience. BYSS... listens to what you want and creates a one-of-a-kind personal experience. BYSS... creates experiences that are very detailed while maintaining creativity. BYSS... strives to be flexible enough to take on any challenge and is determined and organized enough to fit your budget. Let's plan your event!

Specialties: Event Design and Coordination
604.671.4841, becauseyousaidso.net
facebook.com/BecauseYouSaidSo
Twitter: @becauseusaidso

Portrait and lower-left photo by Kari Heese, lower-right photos by Maria Laila Photography

Cathy and Brooke Milne

Q&A

What do you like best about owning a business?
The opportunity to work hard and create something that matters. Being able to influence people in a positive way. Creating unforgettable experiences and the freedom to do so.

Who is your role model or mentor?
Cathy: My daughter because she loves to take on new challenges; she inspires me every day.
Brooke: My parents, who have been my biggest supporters and have never let me give up.

What place inspires you?
Cathy: Canada. It is full of possibilities.
Brooke: Caledon Ski Club, my home away from home.

Better Your Best Coaching

Vancouver, British Columbia

Pro-active. Fun. Community-oriented.
Better Your Best is an action-oriented business and lifestyle coaching company that supports their clients to dream, believe and achieve! Better Your Best works with athletes, executives and entrepreneurs to identify champagne goals, create strategic personal or business plans and connect with the right people to achieve success as they define it.

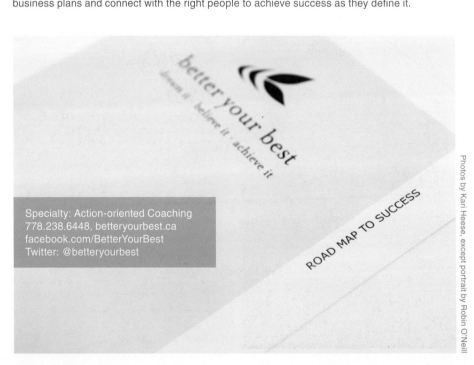

Specialty: Action-oriented Coaching
778.238.6448, betteryourbest.ca
facebook.com/BetterYourBest
Twitter: @betteryourbest

Carolyn de Voest

Q&A

What tip would you give women who are starting a business?
Don't be afraid to fail! Learning through action is instrumental to moving forward, especially in business.

What do you like best about owning a business?
Playing by your own rules! I enjoy having the flexibility to work when I want and where I want. My success is completely dependent on my own efforts.

What is your motto or theme song?
"Don't Stop Believing" by Journey; I know, super cheesy! Don't stop believing is just a great reminder that our biggest obstacles are usually ourselves.

Jillian Bice

Q&A

What are your most popular
products or services?
Our bloom Essentials! We've taken out
a lot of the guesswork by offering only
luxury adult accessories selected for
their beauty, superior engineering, smart
functionality and quality of materials used.

What do you like best about
owning a business?
Being independent, feeling challenged
and driven, setting a great example
for my daughters and knowing I'm
making very good use of my days.

How do you relax?
Soothing massage, yummy wine, great
conversation and deep sleep. In any order
and best done with someone I love.

bloom

Vancouver, British Columbia

Sexy. Healthy. Smart.
bloom believes that sexual knowledge is power and pleasure a birthright. Combining luxury products with the latest trends, tips and techniques, and informative articles, bloom gives women the ability to explore and celebrate their sexuality. bloom's online boutique makes discrete shopping so simple. Chic, savvy and definitely au courant, visit bloom at bloomenjoyyourself.com, where smart women are invited to learn, love their bodies and bloom.

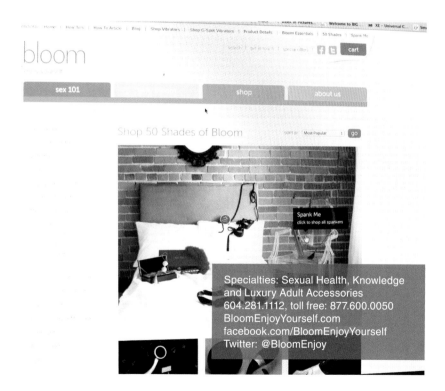

Specialties: Sexual Health, Knowledge and Luxury Adult Accessories
604.281.1112, toll free: 877.600.0050
BloomEnjoyYourself.com
facebook.com/BloomEnjoyYourself
Twitter: @BloomEnjoy

25

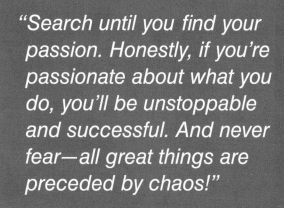

"Search until you find your passion. Honestly, if you're passionate about what you do, you'll be unstoppable and successful. And never fear—all great things are preceded by chaos!"

—Jillian Bice of bloom

Body Exchange

Vancouver, Surrey, Langley, Maple Ridge,
North Shore and Burnaby

Empowering. Life-changing. Fearless.
Body Exchange is Canada's only fitness and adventure company dedicated to the plus size community. The unique concept of Body Exchange offers an inviting, supportive environment for women to improve their health with a tribe of their own. Body Exchange is on the move, serving the plus size market in six locations with a solid platform for further expansion through licensing. Changing lives, perceptions and attitudes since 2008.

Louise Green

Q&A

What makes your business unique?
Few businesses share our focus. Plus
size women have been trying to fit into the
mainstream fitness model for decades.
We understand that for some, there are
different physical and psychological
needs in finding fitness success and
that not everyone fits into one mold.

What do you like best about
owning a business?
I love that I can be creative and
watch my business grow and evolve
as well as having the freedom to
raise my son on my terms.

What motivates and inspires you?
People who defy the norm and overcome
adversity really inspire me; I am deeply
motivated and inspired by watching the
women I work with change their lives.

Specialties: Fitness, Adventure
and Destination Retreats
Plus Size Exclusive
604.785.7018, bodyexchange.ca
facebook.com/TheBodyExchange
Twitter: @BodyExchange

Nicole Ritchie-Oseen

Q&A

What are your most popular products or services?
One of our best-selling styles are our Canadian-made Yoga Jeans. They are truly the most comfortable, and addictive, denim!

What do you like best about owning a business?
The work I do is ultimately about making necessary changes to the fashion industry. I also simply adore helping women feel great about themselves! The clothes are the icing.

What motivates you on a daily basis?
Stubborn determination, and realizing I'm doing something that I'm good at and that I really enjoy.

body politic

Main Street, Vancouver

Emboldened. Lasting. Contemporary.

body politic began as a neighbourhood boutique in Vancouver, fulfilling the need for a well-curated selection of ethical and organic clothing and accessories. Quickly, demand stretched beyond the bricks-and-mortar store, resulting in the creation of an online storefront with customers stretching across North America. Today, body politic is a trusted source of the best contemporary eco-collections, satisfying its mandate of "sustainable design, limitless style."

208 E 12th Ave, Vancouver, 604.568.5528
bodypolitic.ca
facebook.com/bodypoliticboutique
Twitter: @body_politic

Photos by Kari Heese

> *"Give your business time to grow and yourself time to learn!"*
>
> —Nicole Ritchie-Oseen of body politic

Photo by Kari Heese

Clio de la Llave

Q&A

What are your most popular products or services?
Social media management and strategy development.

What do you like best about owning a business?
My ability to chose a strong team and see the things we are able to achieve together.

What is your biggest fear?
Making the same mistake twice.

What motivates you on a daily basis?
Making our clients happy and making sure that our work directly relates to their constant growth.

What is your motto or theme song?
Make genuine and lasting relationships to see the best results.

Booje Media

Vancouver, British Columbia

Innovative. Viral. Authentic.

Booje Media promotes business brands using social media. They help companies and brands find a voice online and create relationships with targeted audiences so that they can hear what people are saying about their brand. They help find creative ways to stand out from their competitors and emulate their business image online.

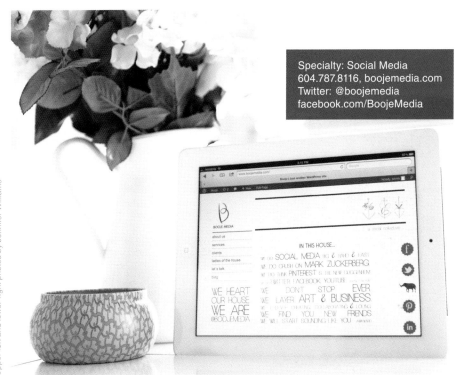

Specialty: Social Media
604.787.8116, boojemedia.com
Twitter: @boojemedia
facebook.com/BoojeMedia

Upper-left and lower-right photos by Jennifer Williams

"Don't ever limit yourself. You'll be surprised what you can do."

—Clio de la Llave of Booje Media

Kari Heese

Q&A

What are your most popular products or services?
Boudoir sessions are very popular. Perfect for a bride or any woman who wants to celebrate her beauty and capture it through intimate images.

What motivates you on a daily basis?
My clients. I love being able to watch someone look at his or her images for the first time. I see the whole range of emotions; it is pretty amazing.

What is your motto or theme song?
"Life isn't about waiting for the storm to pass. It's about learning to dance in the rain." It's important to live, learn and love every day.

Specialty: Wedding and Portrait Photography
604.558.4848
boutiquestudios.ca
facebook.com/boutiquestudios
Twitter: @boutiqueboudoir

Boutique Studios

Vancouver, British Columbia

Classic. Timeless. Intimate.
Boutique Studios focuses on creating contemporary wedding, portrait and boudoir images for discerning clientele. Award-winning photographer Kari Heese and her team collaborate with clients to establish a comfortable, personable relationship. With an emphasis on exceptional customer service, every experience with Boutique Studios is as unique as the timeless images that clients treasure.

Photos by Kari Heese

Brooklyn Designs

Vancouver, British Columbia

Modern. Feminine. Timeless.
Brooklyn Designs is an in-demand jewellery label designed by Brooke Mosher,
featuring delicate nature-inspired jewelry that can be transformed from day to night.
Designed with sophistication, Brooklyn Designs has many options for any modern
bride and her party that can be worn for years after that special day. Their jewels
have been seen on major television shows and are sold in boutiques and online.

Specialties: 14kt Gold-filled and
Sterling Silver Jewelry
brooklyndesigns.ca
facebook.com/BrooklynDesigns
Twitter: @brklyndesigns

Opposite page: portrait and upper-left
photo by Vairdy Photography

Q&A

Brooke Mosher

What are your most popular products or services?
Our nature-inspired jewels are very popular. Pieces with leaves and feathers always sell out. The colours of the ocean are also very attractive to our customers.

What tip would you give women who are starting a business?
Trust yourself and believe in your product/service. Know who your customer is and listen to them.

What do you like best about owning a business?
Everything! I like owning my responsibilities and having to answer to myself.

What is your motto or theme song?
"Got to be true to myself." —Ziggy Marley

Nada Vuksic

Q&A

What are your most popular
products or services?
Unusual and beautiful frames from around
the world and hi-tech lenses including the
newest digital products. And our overall
customer service is second to none.

What tip would you give women
who are starting a business?
Expect to work harder than you've
ever worked before! Believe in your
product or service, and listen. A
client who complains wants to stay a
client; otherwise they disappear.

What do you CRAVE?
A better world, the ability to give back
and lots of shoes. *Lots* of shoes.

bruce eyewear inc.

Gastown, Vancouver

Helpful. Modern. Amazing.
bruce eyewear is different... their frame/sunglasses collection has been carefully curated to be modern, edgy *and* timeless. Their technical knowledge is superior and clients are not just a demographic, but interesting people who want to look and see their very best! The licensed opticians are opinionated (in an honest way) and helpful... just keep an open mind. Shopping here is fun!

Specialty: Original Eyewear
219 Abbott St, Vancouver, 604.662.8300
bruceeyewear.com

Busy Bump
Maternity Services

Vancouver, British Columbia

Resourceful. Thorough. Supportive.
Busy Bump Maternity Services is a baby planning service for expectant mothers, offering a variety of packages, a la carte services and workshops to help prepare for baby's arrival. Becoming a new parent can be overwhelming! Busy Bump will help you with all the essentials to make the transition to parenthood as smooth as possible.

Stephanie Lauzon

Q&A

What are your most popular products or services?
The Ultimate Baby Planning package and Baby Gear 101 package. We also have friends and family of expectant couples purchase gift certificates toward our services and custom gift baskets!

What tip would you give women who are starting a business?
Fully commit yourself to planning, researching and developing your business. When you put your everything into it, the sense of accomplishment when it is a success feels amazing!

What do you CRAVE?
Happiness, health, time with family and a closet full of shoes!

Specialties: Baby Planning
604.575.4555, busybump.com
facebook.com/busybump, Twitter: @BusyBump

"When you find something you are passionate about and love doing, it doesn't feel like work!"

—Stephanie Lauzon of
Busy Bump Maternity Services

Caroline Calvert

Q&A

What are your most popular products or services?
Web design services and search engine optimization (SEO).

What tip would you give women who are starting a business?
Write a business plan and have a cash flow work sheet that you check into at least once a week.

What do you like best about owning a business?
The freedom to make my own decisions and plan my time.

Who is your role model or mentor?
My amazing girlfriends who are creative and inspiring.

What motivates you on a daily basis?
My husband who is always so motivated and has inspired me and encouraged me to follow my dreams.

How do you relax?
Going for a pedicure and massage.

What place inspires you?
Stepping away from my daily routine and going camping with my husband and kids. There is nothing more inspiring than getting out of the city and into the wilderness.

What do you CRAVE?
A glass of wine and my mom's spaghetti.

Caroline Calvert Creative

Vancouver, British Columbia

Professional. Knowledgeable. Innovative.
Caroline Calvert Creative is a full-service web design and social media management company for small business. Caroline Calvert offers graphic design services, search engine optimization, web design and website maintenance. Knowing what small businesses need, she provides the tools and knowledgeable advice that give her clients a worry-free experience when creating their online identity.

Specialties: Web Design and Development
604.868.9189, carolinecalvertcreative.com
facebook.com/carolinecalvertcreative
Twitter: @carolinecalvert

Rhonda Davis

Q&A

What are your most popular
products or services?
Consignment, a free wardrobing service
called a "Diva Den," after-hours shopping,
our daily VIP Facebook and Twitter
codes, our monthly e-newsletter and
our two annual fashion show events.

What tip would you give women
who are starting a business?
When I signed my first lease, a mentor
of mine who owns retail stores said,
"You have chosen a very difficult path."
It is true. Being resilient is a must.

What do you like best about
owning a business?
I like the autonomy to chart the path that
I want my business to take. I like being
an important part of the community
and rocking people's worlds, daily.

Changes Clothing & Jewellery Bar

West Point Grey, Vancouver

Inspiring. One-of-a-kind. Trailblazing.
Changes Clothing & Jewellery Bar took Vancouver by storm in 1997 by offering a mix of new and like-new, trendy women's designer clothing, along with a jewellery bar that sparkles with local and Canadian designers' creations. Long known as a pillar of Point Grey Village, Changes continues to wow clients with over 200 daily arrivals, outstanding consignment, 14 annual events and amazing service.

Specialties: Consignment and Jewellery Bar
4454 W 10th Ave, Vancouver, 604.222.1505
changesclothing.com
facebook.com/ChangesVancouverFanClub
Twitter: @ChangesGood
ca.linkedin.com/in/rhondadeedavis

Photos by Vairdy Photography

Cherlyn Skincare

Vancouver, British Columbia

Nourishing. Courageous. Honest.

With the philosophy that skin needs love, attention and nutrients, the goal at Cherlyn Skincare is to nourish a woman's skin, body, mind and heart. Cherlyn Skincare uses only 100 percent natural and body-friendly ingredients with no synthetic fragrances, toxic preservatives or animal testing. Cherlyn Skincare enjoys providing high-quality products that help women feel good about themselves in every way. Made in Vancouver, Canada.

Specialty: Skin Care
604.733.5200, cherlyn.ca
facebook.com/Cherlyn.Skincare
Twitter: @CherlynSkincare

Cherlyn

Q&A

What tip would you give women who are starting a business?
Learn and grow in ways that you didn't think were possible, be willing to go through fear, have passion for what you do and appreciate everyone who helps you succeed.

What motivates you on a daily basis?
I am motivated to change women's lives for the better. I want to encourage women (and men) to believe that they are beautiful inside and out, no matter what anyone says!

What place inspires you?
The beach, where I go and write in my journal to ground myself and look at the beautiful scenery. I am extremely grateful to live in Vancouver.

LIVE *Well*

LOVE *Much*

LAUGH *Often*

"I love being creative, making my own decisions and learning new skills that allow me to grow. Best of all, I love making a positive difference in this world!"

—Cherlyn of Cherlyn Skincare

Cutie Pie Wax Bar

Vancouver, British Columbia

Friendly. Caring. Talented.
Keep Calm and Wax On! Cutie Pie Wax Bar lives and breathes waxing. These cuties are total clean freaks and adhere to the highest levels of hygiene, including no double dipping. They are dedicated to taking this intimate experience and making it fun. Their bubbly and talented wax experts specialize in Brazilians so that you can rest assured that your goodies are in good hands.

Specialty: Brazilian Waxing
15-636 Clyde Ave, West Vancouver, 604.912.0131
112 - 223 Mountain Hwy, North Vancouver, 604.929.2202
cutiepiewaxbar.com, facebook.com/cutiepiewaxbar
Twitter: @cutiepiewaxbar

Photos by Jennifer Williams

Lindsay Brown

Q&A

What tip would you give women
who are starting a business?
Facing the parts of business that scare you
will teach you the most about yourself.

What do you like best about
owning a business?
The opportunity to provide our clients with
a fun and comfortable waxing experience.
Our clients leave full of confidence and
smooth as butter. That's what I like.

What place inspires you?
My grandparent's cottage! I love the
vintage wallpaper, china tea cups
and that home-away-from-home
feeling. I brought that to Cutie Pie.

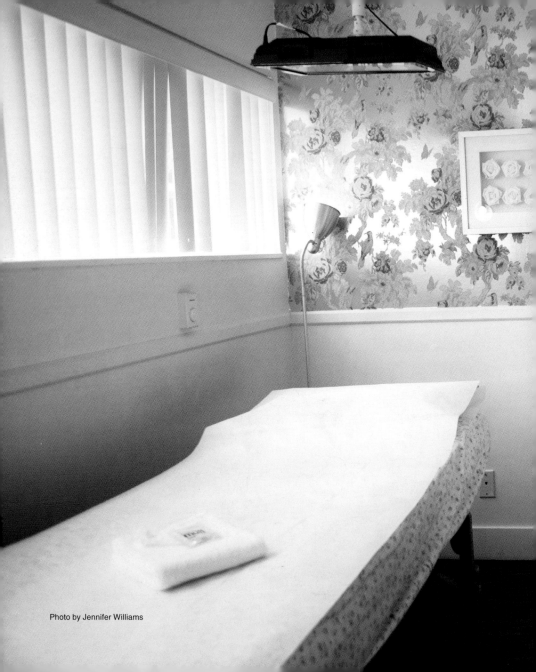

Photo by Jennifer Williams

"I crave adventure, creativity and awesome experiences."

—Lindsay Brown of Cutie Pie Wax Bar

The Dailey Method

Dunbar Village, Vancouver

Fun. Effective. Efficient.
The Dailey Method is a unique combination of ballet barre work, core conditioning, muscle strengthening, yoga and orthopedic exercises. This challenging one-hour class strengthens, tones and lengthens the entire body. All movement is focussed, effective and safe. Proper alignment is the primary focus. Each set of exercises is followed by a series of active stretches to develop more sculpted muscles. Through this process one's body, posture and physical awareness is transformed.

Specialties: Compassion, Health, Transformation
3584 W 41st Ave, Vancouver, 604.266.9191
Child-minding is available Mon–Fri, 9:40am, 11am
thedaileymethod.com, Twitter: @TDMVancouver
facebook.com/TheDaileyMethodVancouver

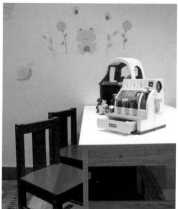

Karen and Jey Wyder

Q&A

What are your most popular products or services?
Our Principles class: an ideal for newcomers to The Dailey Method and for experienced clients who want a truly focussed workout. Also, those who auto-pay monthly get extra perks.

Who is your role model or mentor?
Jill Dailey: love yourself and others. Chip Wilson: set goals. Pam Weiss: listen with heart, body and mind. Darrell Kopke: have fun! Barb Crompton: be smart and take care of people. Clark Bentall: integrity.

How do you relax?
The Dailey Method, walks in nature, looking at the mountains, sky and ocean. We also love to reward ourselves at the Fairmont Pacific Rim spa.

Photo by Jennifer Williams

"*Being of service in our community motivates us.*"

—Karen and Jey Wyder of The Dailey Method

Design Project

Vancouver, British Columbia

Fresh. Accessible. Inspiring.

In a world where "interior design" is usually reserved for the wealthy elite, Design Project offers custom interior decorating to suit every budget. Design Project is committed to making great decor both accessible and realistic, while never sacrificing quality, warmth and style. From custom paint-colour selection to original artwork by Missy, or even a full overhaul, no project is too big or too small.

Q&A

Missy Geiger

What tip would you give women who are starting a business?
Don't be afraid: if you want it, people will be able to see your passion and will trust in it!

What do you like best about owning a business?
The freedom to be creative in the ways that I love, and the reward when my clients are happier in their homes!

Who is your role model or mentor?
My mom. Not only does she work hard, but she makes every guest in her home feel like family. Her view of the sacred nature of "home" is so inspiring.

What is your motto or theme song?
If you want what you have never had, you have to do what you have never done.

Specialties: Interiors and Custom Artwork
604.800.4126
designproject.ca
facebook.com/DesignProjectVancouver
linkedin.com/in/designproject
Twitter: @vancitydesign

Dhahan Law
Barristers, Solicitors and Notaries Public
www.dhahanlaw.com

Jordana A. Dhahan
Barrister, Solicitor & Notary Public

Dhahan Law
1058 - 2560 Shell Road, Richmond, BC V6X 0B8
604-375-9976

jordana@dhahanlaw.com

Jordana Dhahan

Q&A

What tip would you give women
who are starting a business?
Don't be afraid to do things differently
than your industry does. Your
uniqueness can be the way forward.

What motivates you on a daily basis?
The opportunity to connect with people
and create something greater than
the sum of its parts. My practice is
not just business. It's an opportunity
to create and connect with people.

What is your motto or theme song?
"Every small thing makes a difference"
is my motto, whether it's professionally,
socially or personally. Of course,
the big things matter too!

Dhahan Law

South Granville, Vancouver, and Bridgeport, Richmond

Experienced. Strategic. Flexible.

Dhahan Law offers a unique approach by tailoring its services, meeting locations, hours, and billing structures to client needs. Plus, there are no hidden fees. Dhahan Law reduces, reuses, and recycles to be cost-efficient for clients and resource-efficient for our planet. Dedicated to client convenience and strategic solutions, Dhahan Law takes matters off your hands and turn problems into progress.

Specialties: Law and Notary Services
By appointment only:
506 - 1625 W 13th Ave, Vancouver
1058 - 2560 Shell Rd, Richmond
604.375.9976, jordana@dhahanlaw.com

Photos by Kari Heese

Divine Intervention Inc.

Vancouver, British Columbia

Custom. Discerning. Discreet.
Divine Intervention is a boutique, relationship-oriented, high-end matchmaking and dating service specializing in executives, business owners, professionals and artists. As one of Canada's leading matchmakers, Divine Intervention pulls out all the stops to help clients lay the groundwork for successful long-term relationships. Divine conducts custom searches for its clients and prescreens all potential matches. Quality trumps quantity!

Specialties: Matchmaking &
Love Coaching
604.488.0866
divinematchmaking.ca
facebook.com/Divinematchmaking
Twitter: @susansemeniw
linkedin.com/in/susansemeniw-
matchmaker

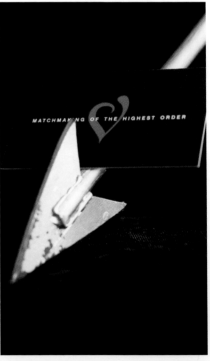

MATCHMAKING OF THE HIGHEST ORDER

Photos by Karl Heese

Susan Semeniw

Q&A

What are your most popular products or services?
A custom matchmaking search.

What tip would you give women who are starting a business?
Make sure you have passion, perseverance and a willingness to adapt to market conditions.

What do you like best about owning a business?
Pride in my work and the flexibility.

Who is your role model or mentor?
People who have overcome adversity.

What motivates you on a daily basis?
The ability to help others and jump-start someone's love life.

What is your motto or theme song?
Under-promise and over-deliver.

How do you relax?
Rollerblading, exercising, spending time with friends and family, getting out of town and being pampered.

What place inspires you?
The Caribbean because it's serene and peaceful. Paris because it's the city of love and has so much to offer.

What do you CRAVE?
Excellence.

Alisha Chand

Q&A

What tip would you give women who are starting a business?
Do something you really love. Nurture it. Be organized and do your research so that you are prepared for whatever comes your way. Above all, be gutsy!

What do you like best about owning a business?
I can create my own unique style.

What is your motto or theme song?
My theme song is "Upgrade U" by Beyoncé. Confident, strong, smart. The song embodies all of those things in a kind of cheeky way.

How do you relax?
Watching hockey!

Fancy That Event Styling

Vancouver, British Columbia

Sophisticated. Glamorous. Classic.
With influences from around the world, Fancy That Event Styling focuses on creating lasting memories through intricate details such as custom floral arrangements, handmade party favours and custom candy buffets. Whether it be for wedding showers, sweet 16s or corporate launches, Fancy That Event Styling is bringing glamour back one party at a time.

Specialties: Custom Candy Buffets, Personalized Party Favours, Edible Decor
604.619.3096, fancythatstyling.com

Photos by Jennifer Williams and Andrea Warner

Favourite Gifts

North Vancouver

Handmade. Inspiring. Collaborative.
Favourite Gifts is an independent designer collective located in the Lonsdale Quay Market in beautiful North Vancouver. Since opening in 2006, Favourite Gifts has showcased a carefully curated selection of locally made clothing, jewellery, accessories and gifts for all occasions. The artists featured at Favourite Gifts take turns working in the store, so you might just find your favourite local designer behind the counter!

Q&A

Carol Hyslop

You might be surprised to know...
Collective members take turns working in the store, which gives our customers the opportunity to meet and build relationships with their favourite local designers and maybe even order a custom piece!

What tip would you give women who are starting a business?
Trust your instincts, and whatever you do, do it with passion and integrity.

What motivates you on a daily basis?
The amazingly talented artists and designers who I work with every day are constantly inspiring... I want to share their incredible creations with the world.

Specialties: Unique Gifts and Accessories Handmade with Love
Lonsdale Quay Market, 2nd Level
204 - 123 Carrie Cates Ct, North Vancouver, 604.904.8840
favouritegifts.ca, facebook.com/favouritegifts
Twitter: @favouritegifts

Q&A

Catherine Lalonde

What are your most popular products or services?
Everyone loves our custom goody bags and DIY beauty kits, with which the girls can make their very own beauty products from natural ingredients. Our mother/daughter spa experiences are popular too.

What tip would you give women who are starting a business?
Sacrifice and be patient, pour your heart into your work, keep a positive attitude and energy, live with passion and purpose, challenge your fears and follow your dreams.

Who is your role model or mentor?
My mother. She's always been true to herself and always encouraged me to find freedom in following my heart, being my own person and doing what I love most.

Feel Fabulous Mobile Spa

Vancouver, British Columbia

Fun. Girly. Educational.
Feel Fabulous Mobile Spa specializes in spa birthday parties for kids and teens, with operations in Vancouver, Edmonton and Calgary. They offer a one-of-a-kind home-spa experience with customized invitations, cozy and colourful spa decor, music, fabulous spa and beauty services, beauty product-making activities and glamorous goody bags that Mom can be proud to give away!

Specialty: Event Planning
604.568.6800, feelfabulous.ca
facebook.com/feelfabulousmobilespa
Twitter: @feelfabulousspa
linkedin.com/in/lalondecatherine

"Life isn't about finding yourself.
Life is about creating yourself."

—Catherine Lalonde of Feel Fabulous Mobile Spa

Filou Designs

Vancouver, British Columbia

Canadian. Independent. Handcrafted.
Filou Designs features original nature-inspired sterling silver and mixed-media
jewellery designs created by artist Fiona Louie in signature cutout silhouette,
medallion, and 3-D styles. Each piece is like a tiny sculpture of wearable art. Find that
special piece for everyday wear, to layer on dressy occasions or for a treasured gift.
Adorn yourself with jewels that mean something. Which piece speaks to you?

Specialties: Nature-Inspired Jewellery
604.728.0239, filoudesigns.com
facebook.com/filoudesigns, Twitter: @filoudesigns

Photos by Vairdy Photography

Fiona Louie

Q&A

What are your most popular
products or services?
Necklaces are popular in a variety
of designs. Everyone has her story
on how the piece is special to her
and symbolizes a part of her life.

What tip would you give women
who are starting a business?
Visualize your goal: where you would
like to end up and how you would
like your life to be... then be prepared
to work hard to pave that path!

What do you like best about
owning a business?
I find it rewarding to see the business grow
and to watch ideas become a reality.

Upper-left and lower-right photos by Jeremy Lim Photography

Forum for Women Entrepreneurs (FWE)

Downtown Vancouver

Bold. Dynamic. Engaging.

The Forum for Women Entrepreneurs (FWE) is a place for women entrepreneurs to get tough questions answered. Offerings include E-series, providing comprehensive entrepreneurial education, connections and support to high-growth companies; the Mentor Program and Member Forums; and seriously fun events. FWE is dedicated to providing visionary entrepreneurs with the knowledge, support and connections they need to become wildly successful.

Q&A

Christina Anthony,
Founder & Chair

What tip would you give women
who are starting a business?
Understand how you are going to make
money and stick with a focused plan.
Always remember to have fun, and if
something is not working, change it.

What do you like best about
owning a business?
The ability to adapt.

What motivates you on a daily basis?
The energy and determination
displayed by the women
entrepreneurs in our community.

What place inspires you?
The FWE Annual Gala celebration,
when more than 450 men and
women come together to celebrate
the successes of entrepreneurs.

Specialties: Education, Mentorship
1208 - 409 Granville St, Vancouver, 604.682.8115
FWE.CA, facebook.com/FWEBC
Twitter: @fwebc, linkedin.com/in/fwebc

Hagensborg
Chocolates Ltd.

Burnaby, British Columbia

Whimsical. Yummy. Natural.
In a chocolate kingdom located in Burnaby, Canada, the reigning princess, assisted
by her team of princesses-in-waiting, produces the finest European chocolates in
all the land. Truffle Pigs and Kiss Me Frogs are made with only the finest European
ingredients master crafted and sold throughout Canada, the United States and Japan.
All subjects have fallen under the spell of her magical, award-winning recipes.

Specialties: Fine European Chocolates
103 - 3686 Bonneville Pl, Burnaby, 604.215.0234
hagensborg.com, Twitter: @trufflepigbar

Photos by Joanna Moss

Shelley Wallace

Q&A

What are your most popular
products or services?
Truffle Pig Bars and Wild Boar Bars.

What tip would you give women
who are starting a business?
Hang on!

What do you like best about
owning a business?
The versatility and the fact that
there is never a ceiling!

Who is your role model or mentor?
Audrey Hepburn.

What motivates you on a daily basis?
My kids, my staff and the love for what I do.

Jennifer Abbott

✦ Hear at Home ✦
MOBILE HEARING CLINIC LTD.

Q&A

What are your most popular
products or services?
Offering a mobile service as well as
a variety of hearing aid options is
what makes us positively unique!

What do you like best about
owning a business?
I am not restricted when it
comes to being creative.

What is your biggest fear?
My biggest fear would be having to go
and work for someone else again.

How do you relax?
Sunday mornings in bed with a
hot cup of tea and newspaper! I
look forward to this quiet time!

Hear at Home Mobile Hearing Clinic LTD

North Vancouver, British Columbia

Healthy. Helpful. Comfortable.
Hear at Home was founded by Jennifer Abbott, who has a passion for offering her clients good old-fashioned customer service. Hear at Home is the only 100 percent mobile clinic in BC. Hear at Home tests individuals in their own environment where they are able to make a personal assessment of each person's real-life listening needs.

Specialties: Hearing Testing, Fitting Hearing Aids
149-1233 Lynn Valley Rd, North Vancouver
778.340.1101
hearathome.com
facebook.com/mobilehearingclinic
Twitter: @hearathome
ca.linkedin.com/in/jenniferabbott

Photo by Kari Heese

"Start a business that ignites passion within; that way the work you do will be gratifying and not really seem like work at all!"

—Jennifer Abbott of Hear at Home Mobile Hearing Clinic LTD

Carrie Dhensaw

Q&A

What are your most popular products or services?
Our 75-liter moving crate, which is manufactured in Canada from 95 percent recycled plastic and has a life span of 10–12 years. Our oldest crates, from 2006, are still moving families.

What tip would you give women who are starting a business?
Listen, without judgment, seek knowledge and strive to become the authority in your field.

What is your motto or theme song?
"Never too late, never too bad, never too old, never too sick to start from scratch all over again." —Bikram Choudhury

It's Your Move

Vancouver, British Columbia

Genuine. Smart. Flexible.

Countering the myth that eco-friendly products and services come at a cost disincentive, It's Your Move encourages consumers to "think outside the cardboard box" by promoting a convenient, cost-effective and eco-friendly alternative to the use of wasteful cardboard boxes for moving. It's Your Move provides a rental service of heavy-duty reusable moving crates and supplies throughout the Lower Mainland and Fraser Valley.

Specialty: Sustainable Moving Crates and Supplies
604.835.7225, saynotoboxes.com, Twitter: @saynotoboxes

Photos by Jennifer Williams

This page photos by Dejan Milicevic. Opposite page: upper photo by Patrick Parenteau, lower-right photo by Gordan Dumka

Jacqueline Conoir
Boutique and Studio

Olympic Village, Vancouver

Edgy. Confident. Glamorous.
Jacqueline Conoir Boutique and Studio is a locally run clothing store. They carry two lines: Jacqueline Conoir embodies strong, driven and accomplished women who are not afraid to be noticed, and JAC is about the "rock star" in all of us. The brand personality is edgy, provocative and cool. The JAC woman is connected and inspired by true city living.

Q&A

Rozemerie Cuevas

What tip would you give women who are starting a business?
I have learned over the years that to survive in business, it takes stamina, determination, focus, willpower and surrounding yourself with people who care and are behind you all the way.

What do you like best about owning a business?
Wearing different hats: I can help with marketing strategies or sales and research fabrics from around the world as well as design.

Who is your role model or mentor?
Young designers with their determination push me every day. Established designers, such as Donna Karan and Tom Ford, who have evolved and grown with the market trends.

Specialty: Premium Women's Clothing Brands
164 West 5th Ave, Vancouver, 604.688.5222, jacquelineconoir.com
facebook.com/JacquelineConoir, Twitter: @JAC_Lines
JAC by Jacqueline Conoir: jacline.com, facebook.com/jacline.fashion

Jennifer Williams Boudoir Photography

Yaletown, Vancouver

Chic. Sensual. Evocative.
A boudoir session with Jennifer Williams is an experience that will change the way you see yourself. With beautiful use of light, natural retouching and gorgeous expressions, she will create timeless images that you will be proud of and can enjoy for years to come. Jennifer's studio is located in Vancouver, however, she has been commissioned by women in many major cities around the world.

Specialty: Boudoir Photography
857 Beatty St, Vancouver, 604.259.4488
jenniferwilliams.com, Twitter: @boudoir_studio
facebook.com/JenniferWilliamsBoudoirStudio

Photos by Jennifer Williams, except lower-left photo on opposite page by Jenn Best

Jennifer Williams

Q&A

What do you like best about owning a business?
I love the feeling of accomplishment, that I created something really special that other people love and enjoy.

What is your biggest fear?
Not having enough time or resources to seize every opportunity!

What motivates you on a daily basis?
I love having an effect on women's self-perception. Helping them feel beautiful on the outside has quite the impact on how they feel about themselves on the inside.

What place inspires you?
New York City inspires me because I love the people, the scenery and the energy! It's very easy to fall in love with that city.

"*Feel the fear and do it anyway because growth comes from doing things that scare you. There's always a chance that you may fail, but what if you succeed instead?*"

—Jennifer Williams of Jennifer
   Williams Boudoir Photography

Photo by Jennifer Williams

Jive Communications

Vancouver, British Columbia

Savvy. Tailored. Personable.
Jive Communications is a boutique PR agency that delivers results—period.
With offices in both Vancouver and Toronto, Jive handles public relations, social media and corporate communications for some of Canada's top brands. By combining the best mix of communications channels for your business (no, not everybody should be on Twitter), Jive makes sure your brand is everywhere.

Q&A

Almira Bardai and
Lindsay Nahmiache

What tip would you give women
who are starting a business?
Build your team of advisors. They've
been through it and can mentor you along
what's often a difficult path. They'll open
doors for you and be a source of support.

What do you like best about
owning a business?
Creating your own destiny. You're
not limited by others' rules and
restrictions. You're building your
strengths and character and
continually upping your game.

What motivates you on a daily basis?
Jive has fantastic clients. We thrive on
delivering the best, smartest, most creative
and strategic communications possible.

Specialties: Strategic Communications,
PR, Social Media, Brand Launches
604.561.7516, jivecommunications.ca
Twitter: @JivePR
linkedin.com/in/lindsaynahmiache

Photos by Karolina Turek Photography

Karolina Turek Photography

Vancouver, British Columbia

Creative. Fresh. Captivating.
Karolina Turek is a headshot specialist. Her fresh outlook on corporate, actor and performer headshots creates eye-catching images with subjects always looking their best. From shooting international celebrities to Vancouver locals, Karolina's style stands out among the rest. Her key to successful headshots is creating a fun, easygoing and comfortable atmosphere.

Q&A

Karolina Turek

What do you like best about owning a business?
Being able to help others pursue their dreams through photography.

Who is your role model or mentor?
My mom, my best friend. She's been a foster parent for over 20 years and has the biggest heart. Such a beautiful soul. I call her for everything.

What is your motto or theme song?
All you need is love.

How do you relax?
Cuddling up to Piper, my French mastiff, always seems to relax me. She's got the magic touch!

Specialty: Headshots
karolinaturek.com
Twitter: @karolinaturek

"My incredible clients motivate me on a daily basis. My clients are so unique and amazing in their own way. We always have lots of fun!"

—Karolina Turek

Razel Serrano

Q&A

What are your most popular products or services?
Dermalogica Skincare, Yonka Skincare, Jane Iredale mineral makeup. Our own Le Petit Spa Signature Line.

What tip would you give women who are starting a business?
Be diligent and be patient. Listen carefully, pick the good ones and remember the bad ones. Believe in yourself and keep in mind and heart that you will succeed.

Who is your role model or mentor?
My mom is my role model. Nancy Mudford, Le Petit Spa founder and my mentor: She was my life jacket when I dove into business without knowing anything about it.

Le Petit Spa

West Point Grey, Vancouver

Beautiful. Relaxing. Welcoming.
An award-winning neighbourhood day spa, Le Petit Spa is well known for their passionate staff that provide excellent facial treatments, microdermabrasion, relaxation massage, waxing and nail services. Everyone at Le Petit Spa provides excellent customer care and top-notch technical work. They aim for perfection and results-oriented services, making sure that their customers leave Le Petit Spa with the best experience ever.

Specialty: Skincare
3701 W Broadway, Vancouver
604.224.4314, lepetitspa.ca

G.M. COLLIN PARIS

Photo by Kari Heese

"What I like best about owning a business is the opportunities! Having the freedom to deliver my own creativity. And I really enjoy taking care of people around me."

—Razel Serrano of Le Petit Spa

L'nielle Pantoja and LeLe Chan

Q&A

What tip would you give women who are starting a business?
Believe in your company, or no one else will.

What do you like best about owning a business?
The freedom to choose.

Who is your role model or mentor?
Our mother. She was always there when we were growing up, not as astay-at-home mom, but as a great example of an entrepreneurial, work-at-home mom.

What motivates you on a daily basis?
The fact that we're working with people in love, from the vendors and my team who love what they do to clients who want to celebrate their love and commitment.

Lé Soirées
Weddings & Events

Vancouver, British Columbia

Savvy. Elegant. Sophisticated.
Lé Soirées Weddings & Events are passionate party perfectionists, committed to creating elegant events tailored to your distinctive style and unique personality. They produce events that are exquisite and unforgettable.

Specialties: Event Production, Wedding Coordination and Design
778.968.5353, lesoirees.com
facebook.com/lesoirees
Twitter: @lesoirees

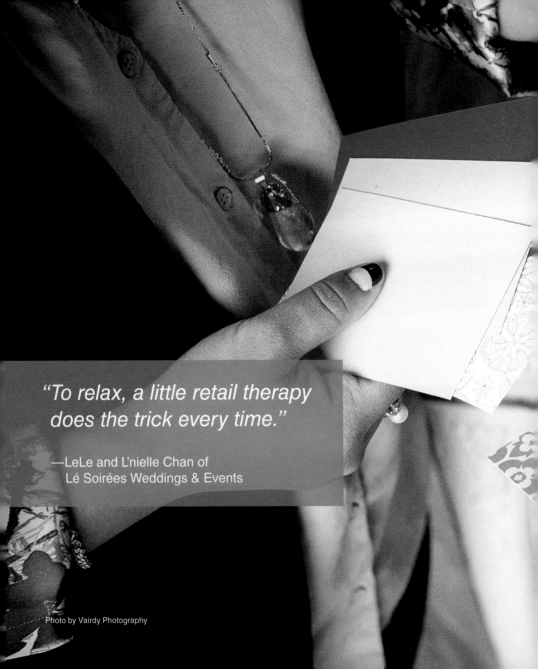

"To relax, a little retail therapy does the trick every time."

—LeLe and L'nielle Chan of
  Lé Soirées Weddings & Events

Photo by Vairdy Photography

Leah Alexandra Jewellery

Vancouver, British Columbia

Timeless. Versatile. Delicate.
Leah Alexandra jewellery offers a timeless elegance that will complement anything from jeans and a T-shirt to a wedding dress. Hand-selected gemstones of all colours are paired with sterling silver and 14k-gold fill, with sea-inspired hues such as turquoise and Peruvian opal being key players. Celebrities such as Jessica Alba have adorned themselves in Leah's jewels. Available at leahalexandra.com, Blue Ruby or The Cross.

Specialties: Timeless Jewellery
604.771.7373, leahalexandra.com
facebook.com/leahalexandrajewellery
Twitter: @LeahAlx_Jewelry

Portrait by Kari Heese

Leah Alexandra

Q&A

What tip would you give women
who are starting a business?
You have to live and breathe it. Absorb
advice from other entrepreneurs. When
things take off, stay humble and try to
maintain a healthy work-life balance.

Who is your role model or mentor?
My parents each have their own
businesses. Their triumphs and
tribulations inspired a strong
work ethic in me. I also had an
entrepreneurial spirit from the get-go.

What motivates you on a daily basis?
After launching a new collection, hearing
from retailers how excited their staff
and customers are is the best! I love
seeing someone wear my jewellery
when they layer several pieces.

Baljit Rayat

Q&A

What tip would you give women
who are starting a business?
I feel it's important to know what your soul's
purpose is, and then create a business
out of it. Living your soul's purpose is
what makes your business successful.

What do you like best about
owning a business?
Being creative and working my own
hours so that I can take the time to
nurture myself, which makes me the
best conduit I can be for my clients.

What is your biggest fear?
That darn fear is one big fat illusion!

What do you CRAVE?
Beauty, abundance, sensuality,
creativity, connection... and chocolate.

Lotus Destiny

Vancouver, British Columbia

Sensual. Creative. Intuitive.

Baljit Rayat is an intuitive soul coach and Akashic Records consultant assisting women in attracting healthy relationships with men, women, body image, money and, most of all, their sensuality. She is the creator and founder of her own healing method called Star Activation™ system, which allows you to discover your soul's purpose, divine gifts and talents, and express them into reality.

Specialty: Intuitive Coaching
baljit@lotusdestiny.com
lotusdestiny.com
facebook.com/lotusdestiny
Twitter: @BaljitRayat
linkedin.com/in/baljitrayat

Photos by Vairdy Photography

Tammy Preast and
Shelly Dueck

Q&A

What are your most popular
products or services?
Loving overnight in-home dog care
while owners are away on vacation. We
tell our clients, "If your dog sleeps on
your bed, you dog will sleep on ours!"

What tip would you give women
who are starting a business?
Find something you are passionate
about and work to make a business
around that passion... in our case,
our passion was our own dogs.

What motivates you on a daily basis?
Each wonderful pooch who comes
through our door steals a piece of
our heart. It motivates us to ensure
that they are happy and healthy and
come back again and again.

Love on a Leash
Trusted Dog Care Services

Vancouver, British Columbia

Reliable. Experienced. Nurturing.
Founded in 2008 by sisters, Tammy Preast and Shelly Dueck, Love on a Leash Trusted Dog Care Services has built up a solid reputation as the company to care for your beloved pooch while you are away! All their caregivers specialize in reliable, responsible and loving in-home care for your dog 365 days a year. Their motto: peace of mind and a happy pooch!

Specialties: Loving Overnight In-home Dog Care
778.552.1301, loveonaleash.ca, Twitter: @loveonaleashbc

Regi Anselmi and
Sally Traynor

Q&A

What are your most popular
products or services?
Our guests love that with our services, they
get a little more: scalp/shoulder and hand
massages, hot towel facial treatments,
makeup touch-ups and aromatherapy.

What tip would you give women
who are starting a business?
Take a leap of faith! If you're a
driven and self-motivated woman,
you can overcome any obstacle!

What do you like best about
owning a business?
The ability to cultivate a positive, fun,
creative environment for our guests,
staff and community. It's very rewarding
to be a destination and gathering
place in our neighbourhood.

Manifesto
Lifestyle Salon

Grandview Woodland, East Vancouver

Creative. Authentic. Collaborative.
The only East side Aveda Concept Salon offering a wide range of naturally focused, aromatherapy-based hair services. Their worldly team allows specialization in current haircut/color techniques for all hair types, men's grooming, up-style and makeup design, editorial and everyday. Book an appointment or just drop by for a cup of tea. They provide an inclusive atmosphere in the most diverse neighborhood in Vancouver.

Specialties: Hair Care, Skincare and Makeup
1126 Commercial Dr, East Vancouver, 604.255.5858
manifestosalon.com, facebook.com/groups/manifestosalon
Twitter: @manifestosalon

Photos by Kari Heese

Modern Mama

Vancouver, British Columbia

Fun. Supportive. Unique.
Modern Mama presents mom-focused events including a nanny service. Events
range from spa days and shopping-with-a-stylist mornings to product giveaways,
parenting workshops, new-mom breakfasts and more. Modern Mama is both an online
and offline community for moms in nine cities in Alberta and British Columbia.

Specialty: Mom-focused Events
604.369.3052, modernmama.com
Twitter: @modern_mama
facebook.com/modernmama

This page: photo by Rhonda Dent. Opposite page: upper-right
photo by Rhonda Dent, lower-right photo by Anita Alberto

Connie Peters

Q&A

What tip would you give women who are starting a business?
Control your spending; start on a shoestring if you can. Save at every turn by bargaining, using free tools like WordPress and utilizing your existing network.

What do you like best about owning a business?
The flexibility it affords me to be there for my kids every day.

What motivates you on a daily basis?
The notion that I can have it all.

What do you CRAVE?
A good book, a night out with friends, a successful event, a great family vacation.

mom inc MOVEMENT

Vancouver, British Columbia

Inspiring. Educational. Supportive.
mom inc MOVEMENT supports and educates moms in all stages of their life
and professional journey. With live events and useful articles, the moms at
mom inc MOVEMENT have a goal to encourage more women to balance their
passion for their families with their passion for their careers. Use their BOSS
directory today to find the business opportunity you have been waiting for.

Julie Nowell,
Meghan Simington
and Christine Nielsen

Q&A

What are your most popular
products or services?
Our BOSS directory. Moms can search
business opportunities in their area
while being educated with the latest
business and lifestyle information.

What tip would you give women
who are starting a business?
Have humility, be open to feedback and
support. Remember it is a marathon,
not a sprint. While multitasking is an
amazing technique, find focus, power
off and recharge sometimes!

What do you like best about
owning a business?
Flexibility and freedom of thought. We
love managing our businesses while
exploring the world with our families.

Specialties: Job Hunting Support and Education for Working Moms
604.992.4203, momincmovement.com
facebook.com/momincmovement, Twitter: @momincmovement

Nina Pousette

Q&A

**What tip would you give women
who are starting a business?**
I would highly recommend finding some
women in business support groups. I am
probably in seven or eight different groups,
and I can't imagine surviving without them!

**What do you like best about
owning a business?**
I love that I can change the way
I run it on a daily basis without
consulting anyone higher up!

What is your biggest fear?
Boredom. It means that I am
not seizing the day!

What motivates you on a daily basis?
I have always been a dreamer. I used to
think that was a bad thing, but now I know
my dreams become my reality! *Dream big!*

Nina Pousette
Realtor® and Chocolatier

Vancouver, British Columbia

Modern. Informative. Conscious.
Nina Pousette is an ingenious entrepreneur who has combined her passion for chocolate with her real estate business as the "Chocolate Realtor," creating a truly unique experience for her clients. Trained as a chocolatier at Le Cordon Bleu Culinary Arts School, Nina worked in Parisian pastry kitchens before starting her artisan chocolate company, My Chocolate Tree, back in Vancouver. Real estate is Nina's way of serving people outside of the kitchen!

Lower-right photo by Jennifer Williams, portrait by Michael Ford

Specialties: Chocolate Goodies and Real Estate Advice
778.994.6654, ChocolateRealEstateAgent.com
facebook.com/NinaPousetteRealtorChocolatier
Twitter: @Choco_Realtor, linkedin.com/in/ninapousette

Nourished

Vancouver, British Columbia

Enlightening. Motivating. Results-driven.
Nourished, a health consulting firm, inspires wellness. One-on-one consultations provide the environment to thrive emotionally and physically. Nourished creates personalized wellness maps to bring more balance, energy, mental clarity, help with weight loss/ management, anxiety and fatigue for life. This isn't a diet, Nourished teaches lifestyle. Nourished provides solutions to live your happiest, most fulfilled life now.

Specialties: Health, Nutrition, Lifestyle Solutions
604.290.1231, nourished.ca
facebook.com/nourished.ca, Twitter: @kittycinc

Photos by Vairdy Photography

Alyssa Bauman

Q&A

I sell health and therefore happiness with my six-month wellness programs, guided cleanses, grocery store tours, workshops and webinars.

Freedom to express who I am on my time. I am completely present in my children's lives. I am my own business so anywhere I go, I am Nourished.

Fresh green juice, acai and hemp smoothies, my daughters' smiles, new places to explore, a killer red lipstick, that lingering kiss, avocados, my native NYC, the perfect little dress.

"*Don't hesitate. Follow your instinct and do it. (Did you know the gut has more neurons than the brain?)*"

—Alyssa Bauman of Nourished

Maryna Bundyuk

Q&A

What do you like best about owning a business?
In running my web design business, I found a perfect synergy for my creative personality, highly cultivated sense of aesthetics, love of coding and need for clarity in all things.

Who is your role model or mentor?
I am fortunate to be learning from Jeffrey Armstrong, an award-winning author who inspires me to bring soul into the workplace and heart into the way we do business.

What place inspires you and why?
I am inspired by discovering. If you really look, you will see the beauty in everything, each aspect of this world has its own inspiration and story. Keep your eyes open.

Opus Talis Designs

Vancouver, British Columbia

Conscious. Passionate. Ingenious.

Opus Talis Designs is an interactive design studio combining branding, web and graphic design, and conscious creativity. In line with the latest technology and passion for purposeful expression, Opus Talis Designs helps their worldwide clientele brand their business and fine-tune their profile, highlighting their brand's integrity and the core values. A team of passionate, fun and unafraid people who don't hesitate to break the codes to lend a freshness to their client's ideas, nurturing each project from the initial hello to the last pixel.

Specialties: Full-service Website Design
604.781.7434, opustalis.com
facebook.com/OpusTalis, Twitter: @marynabundyuk
linkedin.com/in/marynabundyuk

Photos by Vairdy Photography

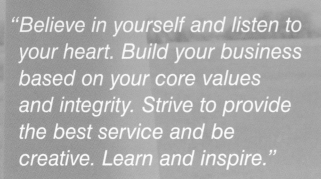

"Believe in yourself and listen to your heart. Build your business based on your core values and integrity. Strive to provide the best service and be creative. Learn and inspire."

—Maryna Bundyuk of Opus Talis Designs

Photo by Vairdy Photography

PEARL
Teeth Whitening Spa

False Creek, Vancouver

Relaxing. Safe. Professional.
PEARL Teeth Whitening Spa offers professional teeth whitening services for anyone looking to brighten up their smile. Relax and feel comfortable in a spalike setting while registered dental hygienists perform your whitening treatment using the highest-quality Canadian-made whitening products. A 40-minute service with immediate results makes your whitening experience easy and effortless. Now that's something to smile about!

Specialty: Teeth Whitening
206 - 1089 W Broadway, Vancouver, 604.742.0046
teethwhiteningbypearl.com, Twitter: @pearlwhitespa

Photos by Jennifer Williams

Shelley Smith

Q&A

What are your most popular
products or services?
Our 40-minute teeth whitening
treatment. With immediate results,
our clients can walk away with a
beautiful smile in less than an hour!

What do you like best about
owning a business?
Having ultimate authority. I can make any
changes and implement any of my ideas
without interference. It's freedom to indulge
in my creative side without restrictions.

What is your biggest fear?
This growing societal pressure
to look young. I want the right to
grow old gracefully, to embrace
wrinkles and age with pride and to
feel my best without surgery.

"Never be afraid to dream big. Just think about where you could be next year at this time if you started today."

—Shelley Smith of PEARL
    Teeth Whitening Spa

Photo by Jennifer Williams

Heather Braun

Q&A

What are your most popular
products or services?
Our clients choose us for our quality
and creativity. We produce the
business card that lands the job, the
invitation that delights and the product
line that inspires your customers.

What tip would you give women
who are starting a business?
Define how you want your business to
work for you so that it supports how you
want to live your life. And go for it.

What do you like best about
owning a business?
A business is a medium through
which to learn and grow. Each day
brings new lessons, new challenges
and new experiences. This insight is
invaluable and incredibly exciting.

Porchlight Press

Mt. Pleasant, Vancouver

Tactile. Clever. Authentic.
Porchlight Press is a one-stop shop for all things freshly letterpressed. The studio thrives on the infinite possibilities of word, imagery and texture. They produce business cards, invitations, packaging, greeting cards, posters, art prints and a wide range of other exquisite paper goods. Let Porchlight Press personalize your project into a beautifully tactile reality.

Specialties: Letterpress Printing, Graphic Design, Paper Goods
204 - 25 E 6th Ave, Vancouver, 604.558.1552
porchlightpress.com, facebook.com/PorchlightPress
Twitter: @porchlightpress

Photo by Ben Haggar

"What motivates me is the thrill of making and sharing with others."

—Heather Braun of Porchlight Press

Jennifer Pedraza

Q&A

What tip would you give women who are starting a business?
Learn everything about your business. You are the only person who will take your business to where you envision it. I found reading books on merchandising, branding and sales helped me.

What do you like best about owning a business?
In my particular business, I love that I am free to be creative. I can make my own schedule, and I'm always surrounded by gorgeous scents.

How do you relax?
Hiking. My husband and I like to take weekends to visit the Olympic Peninsula in Washington State. I also enjoy cooking, photography and a bath with Pure Attar Bath Oils.

Pure Attar
Luxurious Oils

Vancouver, British Columbia

Luxurious. Exotic. Alluring.
Pure Attar Luxurious Oils manufactures and distributes an exclusive line of all-natural products for bath, body, home and spa. Pure Attar products are handcrafted and inspired by the ancient beauty rituals of North Africa, India and the Middle East. Pure Attar Luxurious Oils brings to life Old World beauty secrets, using only the finest botanicals and spices from exotic locations around the world.

Specialties: All-natural Oils for Bath and Body
604.738.9194, pure-attar.com, Twitter: @PureAttar

"The ability to work from anywhere motivates me. Also, the simple fact that I really find joy making my products is meditative for me."

—Jennifer Pedraza of Pure Attar Luxurious Oils

Salon M2 Hair and Skin

Burnaby, British Columbia

Inviting. Modern. Innovative.

At this hot full-service salon, services include hair and aesthetics. The salon is modern, chic and defines luxury. The M2 team has great passion and love for their art. Salon M2 takes pride in doing the "perfect consultation" with each guest by using high-quality products to ensure the perfect look. Each individual will leave with the total package catered to her needs.

Specialties: Hair and Aesthetics
17 - 5901 E Broadway, Burnaby, 604.294.3344
mysalonm2.com
facebook.com/SalonM2, Twitter: @mysalonm2

Photos by Joanna Moss

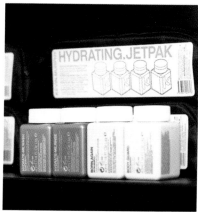

Daniela Macera and
Rosanna Marano

Q&A

What are your most popular
products or services?
Color Foam! Express color for the
working girl who wants a color refresh
in 10 minutes. Love Locks! Great for
introducing new color or spicing up
existing color by adding dimension.

What tip would you give women
who are starting a business?
Put your heart and soul into it. Always
follow your gut and believe in yourself.

What do you like best about
owning a business?
Having the ability to create a wonderful
team that supports what we believe in!

What motivates you on a daily basis?
Each other.

"Stop making excuses: some day is not a day in the calendar."

—Daniela Macera and Rosanna Marano
of Salon M2 Hair and Skin

Saucisse Restaurant

North Vancouver, British Columbia

Upscale. Quality. Delicious.
With a warm, fabulous and sexy vibe, Saucisse Restaurant features premium house dry-aged steaks, unpretentious lunch and dinner menus, an incredible wine list and local craft beer on tap. Popular dishes include sous vide duck confit, house-made duck and macerated blueberry sausages, house-aged steak bar and croque madame. Boasting a lounge and bar, and a beautiful dining room, Saucisse Restaurant delivers an unprecedented dining experience in the heart of the North Shore.

Perienne Sadler

Q&A

What tip would you give women
who are starting a business?
Believe in yourself and truly love what
you do. Starting a business is more than
just a job or a career—it's a lifestyle.

What do you like best about
owning a business?
Our customers choose to spend their
most memorable events and occasions
in our restaurant, eating the food
we've prepared and celebrating with
us. There is no higher compliment.

What place inspires you?
Napa Valley offers the most
incredibly versatile culinary scene
I have ever experienced. It is the
best place to go for inspiration!

Specialty: Upscale French Dining
437 N Dollarton Hwy, North Vancouver, 778.340.1919
SaucisseRestaurant.com, Twitter: @SaucisseRestaur
facebook.com/SaucisseRestaurant.com

"I crave a thriving, empowered, inspired and important local business for my daughters to grow up knowing and never doubting that they can do it all."

—Perienne Sadler of Saucisse Restaurant

Cindy Duric and Barb Mackenzie

Q&A

What tip would you give women who are starting a business?
Do not second-guess yourself. Go with your gut. Believe in yourself. Know that you have something unique to offer.

What do you like best about owning a business?
Having the opportunity to make our ideas realities. We love, and are blessed, to create realities from ideas, concepts and goals.

What place inspires you?
Anywhere new. Experiencing different cultures, vibrant colours, delectable scents and foods, amazing architecture... Italy, Paraguay, Singapore, Switzerland...

What do you CRAVE?
Leaving a memorable mark on the world that will inspire others to do something great for themselves, and helping others do the same. Pay it forward.

Serendipity Event Planning

Vancouver, British Columbia

Soulful. Distinctive. Unforgettable.
From intimate to grand, from weddings and birthdays to anniversaries and baby showers, Serendipity Event Planning loves bringing the passion and creativity to your special occasion. With the passion to create ideas outside of the box, Serendipity's team plays with whimsical concepts and dramatic designs to create memorable, fabulous environments. Serendipity Event Planning: making magical moments one event at a time.

Specialties: Weddings, Birthdays, Baby and Bridal Showers
604.418.1331, serendipityplanners.com
facebook.com/SerendipityPlanning, Twitter: @serendipity604

Shine Nail Bar

Richmond, British Columbia

Shiny. Stylish. Sleek.
Want beautiful nails? At Shine Nail Bar the goal is to make you feel pampered, relaxed and absolutely fabulous by the time you walk out the door. A luxurious yet affordable nail salon located in the heart of Richmond, Shine Nail Bar is serious about nails and committed to hygienic practices.

Lynn Luu

Q&A

What are your most popular
products or services?
Our signature Cocktail Manicure
with with gel polish: chip-free nail
polish that lasts for weeks!

What tip would you give women
who are starting a business?
Follow your intuition. Find a
mentor who inspires you. Feel
passionate about what you do.

Who is your role model or mentor?
Joyce Poon, founder of Noir Lash
Lounge, is inspiring with her
incredible business sense.

What is your motto or theme song?
You can't change yesterday.
Enjoy today. Live for tomorrow.

Specialty: Nail Care
110 - 8228 Westminster Hwy, Richmond, 604.284.5022
shinenailbar.com, facebook.com/shinenailbar
Twitter: @shinenailbar

Photo by Vairdy Photography

"The neighborhood I grew up in inspires me. I visit whenever I can. Every time I leave with appreciation of how far I've come from being a little girl with big dreams."

—Lynn Luu of Shine Nail Bar

Frances Jang, MD, FRCPC

Q&A

What tip would you give women who are starting a business?
Have passion, integrity and understanding of your market; it is hard work most days, and you have to be able to adapt as the business landscape evolves.

What motivates you on a daily basis?
I am motivated by my patients and delivering to their expectations; I enjoy seeing the ancillary benefits of improved self-confidence. I believe that combination treatments (e.g., Botox, lasers, fillers, skincare) are the dawn of a new era; if done in a timely and correct manner, they can truly delay the aging process and perhaps obviate the need for more traditional surgical procedures in future.

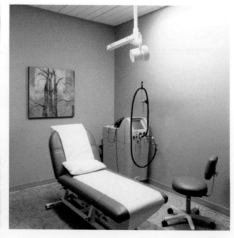

Skinworks

Dunbar, Vancouver

Professional. Knowledgeable. Artistic.
Skinworks is a unique medical clinic featuring two cosmetic specialists, Dr. Nick Carr, head of UBC Plastic Surgery, and Dr. Frances Jang, Dermatologist. Skinworks offers full-spectrum rejuvenation: dermatologically approved skincare products, Botox, fillers, lasers and an operating room fully accredited by the BC College of Physicians. Skinworks won "Best of Vancouver" for four consecutive years, speaking to their high standard of medical care and patient satisfaction.

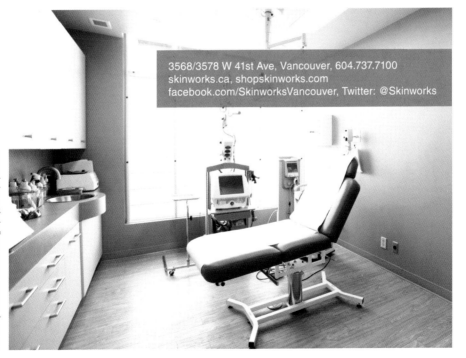

3568/3578 W 41st Ave, Vancouver, 604.737.7100
skinworks.ca, shopskinworks.com
facebook.com/SkinworksVancouver, Twitter: @Skinworks

Amanda Beisel

Q&A

What tip would you give women who are starting a business?
Surround yourself with supportive people who believe in you and your vision. Eliminate any negativity that will distract you from achieving your goal.

What do you like best about owning a business?
I love my clients and being able to help them achieve their skin goals. I have so much gratitude for each and every client.

Who is your role model or mentor?
Vancouver women and their entrepreneurial spirit. Yaletown is filled with inspiring, fierce and determined women business owners. I am so happy to being among this pack of amazing women.

SKN Holistic Rejuvenation Clinic

Yaletown, Vancouver

Innovative. Compassionate. Honest.
SKN Holistic Rejuvenation Clinic is Vancouver's original, natural skincare clinic.
Founded as an alternative to invasive anti-aging clinics, SKN's mission has
always been to provide safe and effective skin treatments that provide clients
with amazing results. SKN continuously researches the latest in skin health
to provide clientele with the most effective and innovative treatments.

Specialties: Natural Skincare
By appointment only: 150 - 1152 Mainland St, Vancouver
604.568.6333, sknclinic.ca
facebook.com/SKNclinic, Twitter: @SKNClinic

Photos by Karolina Turek Photography

Spa Boutique

Kitsilano, Vancouver

Professional. Educational. Knowledgeable.
Spa Boutique is Canada's favorite beauty store specializing in top-quality professional skincare, mineral makeup and nail care. Their Vancouver location is nestled in the heart of Kitsilano and features educational express facials using the skin care brand of their guest's choice. Licensed estheticians are always on staff and happy to provide complimentary consultations and beauty advice.

Specialty: Skincare
3630 W 4th Ave, Vancouver, 604.734.7114
spaboutique.ca, facebook.com/spaboutique
Twitter: @spaboutique
linkedin.com/in/company/spa-boutique

Photos by Kari Heese

Nancy Mudford

Q&A

What tip would you give women
who are starting a business?
Have perseverance for hard work
and focus on finding solutions when
you encounter challenges.

What do you like best about
owning a business?
Flexibility, creativity and the
ability to act quickly on ideas
that I am passionate about.

What place inspires you?
Skiing at the top of Whistler
on a sunny day.

What do you CRAVE?
Financial independence to travel the world
and experience unique adventures.

Photo by Kari Heese

jane iredale
THE SKIN CARE MAKEUP

"Growing my business is very important to me as an entrepreneur. It engages me daily, and meeting goals is addictive."

—Nancy Mudford of Spa Boutique

The Steveston
Cookie Company

Steveston, Richmond

Delicious. Stylish. Original.
The Steveston Cookie Company specializes in gorgeously decorated, melt-in-your-mouth delicious cookies for any occasion. From weddings to corporate gifts to birthday parties, they have your event covered with cookies in any theme your heart desires. Owner Mika Livingston will ensure that each cookie is stylish and perfect for your day. The Steveston Cookie Company is known for its attention to detail, fresh ingredients and original designs.

Mika Livingston

Q & A

What are your most popular products or services?

Custom cookies decorated to match the theme of any special event! Cookie favours make beautiful and fun giveaways at birthday parties, showers, weddings and more!

What tip would you give women who are starting a business?

Do what you love, and do it the best that you can.

What motivates you on a daily basis?

The challenge to provide a product that exceeds expectations. I love it when customers get so excited about the cookies they have ordered.

The Steveston Cookie Company

Specialty: Custom Decorated Cookies
778.297.1597
thestevestoncookiecompany.com
facebook.com/stevestoncookies
Twitter: @stevestoncookie

Beth Fairchild

Q&A

What are your most popular products or services?
Clothing for expectant mothers, baby carriers, diaper bags, fashionable nursing bras and locally made children's clothing.

What tip would you give women who are starting a business?
Do your research, be patient and believe in your venture.

What do you like best about owning a business?
Being in control of my destiny and getting to know people in our community.

What motivates you on a daily basis?
New mothers and their families. I am especially motivated by my own daughter for whom I want to demonstrate hard work.

Steveston Village Maternity

Steveston Village, Richmond

Stylish. Practical. Creative.

Nestled in the quaint community of Steveston Village, this boutique holds more than just stylish and wearable maternity fashion. It is full of baby essentials, nursing products, unique children's fashion and special gifts. Steveston Village Maternity offers a wide selection of locally designed and made merchandise. This shop intrigues the most unexpected passer-by and draws in expectant mothers from across the Lower Mainland.

Specialties: Maternity Fashion, Baby Essentials
110 - 3911 Moncton St, Richmond, 778.297.7379
stevestonvillagematernity.com
facebook.com/stevestonmaternity, Twitter: @svmaternity

Style Nine to Five

Vancouver, British Columbia

Savvy. Resourceful. Innovative.
Style Nine to Five is a fashion career website for Canada with daily job postings such as designer, buyer, PR coordinator, fashion writer, visual merchandiser and more. It's a place where people who want to work in fashion can find amazing opportunities. Fashion jobs are hard to find and often not accessible; Christie Lohr has created a place for employers and job seekers to connect.

Christie Lohr

Q&A

What do you like best about owning a business?
You see direct results from the hard work you put into it. Your workday never ends, so you can go on a hike on a sunny summer afternoon.

What motivates you on a daily basis?
I love the emails I get from job seekers across the country asking for advice, and I get to offer job opportunities to people. It's very rewarding.

How do you relax?
Getting outdoors, working out, shopping, dining out and being with friends.

What do you CRAVE?
A good glass of wine and pushing myself to do bigger and better in life.

Specialty: Fashion Careers
604.314.9158
styleninetofive.com
facebook.com/StyleNineToFive
Twitter: @StyleNineToFive
linkedin.com/in/fashionjobs

Sweet Dreams & Flying Machines

Vancouver, British Columbia

Safe. Functional. Whimsical.
Sweet Dreams & Flying Machines creates the safest form of infant bedding on the market, Baby Sleeping Bags and Swaddles with personality to rally against the sea of pastels and whites. Let them help you get the best, worry-free night's sleep, because trust us—we know how hard a night's sleep is to come by with a little one!

Specialties: Baby Sleeping Bags and Swaddles
604.961.5929
sweetdreamsandflyingmachines.com
facebook.com/SweetDreamsandFlyingMachines

Photos by Kari Heese

Alison Foreman

Q&A

What are your most popular products or services?
Our Dream Sacs: they are the safest form of bedding for infants. They are physically worn and are designed not to bunch up around the face and interfere with breathing.

What motivates you?
My son. I started this business for him and because of him. My line was created because of a gap in the market, and I wanted the flexibility to enjoy these precious years.

What do you CRAVE?
Skiing fast, great snow, windy windsurfing days on the lake, creativity, sunny holidays, family time and hugs from my boys.

Photo by Kari Heese

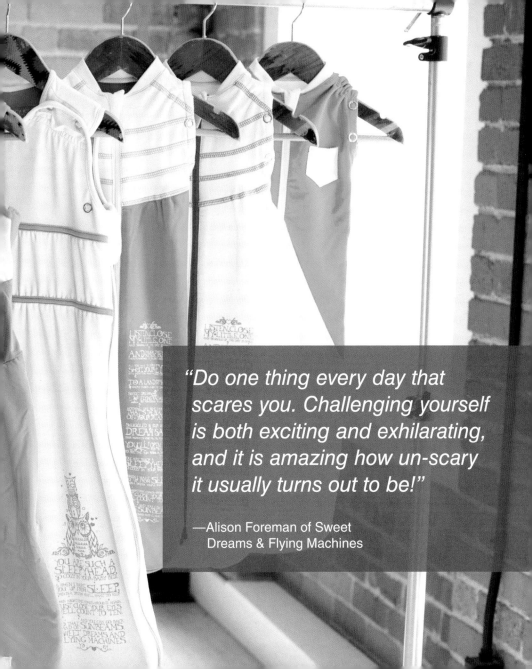

"Do one thing every day that scares you. Challenging yourself is both exciting and exhilarating, and it is amazing how un-scary it usually turns out to be!"

—Alison Foreman of Sweet Dreams & Flying Machines

Toni Sing

Q&A

What are your most popular products or services?
The ability to bring strong negotiating skills to a variety of clientele. Assisting buyers and sellers to make informed decisions about Vancouver real estate.

What tip would you give women who are starting a business?
Always give your best—no matter what. Be prepared to fail more than once; it means you're closer to achieving your goals.

What do you like best about owning a business?
Success is what you make of it. If you work hard, success is inevitable. Learning from your mistakes is a normal part of becoming the best at what you do.

Who is your role model or mentor?
My father. A true businessman and a veteran realtor specializing in Vancouver and Burnaby for over 30 years.

What motivates you on a daily basis?
The positive outcome my clients receive once we have accomplished their goals, whether it be a new home purchase or the sale of their property. There's nothing better.

What do you CRAVE?
Quality time with friends, family and my dogs. It doesn't matter where, just as long as it's there. The time spent with loved ones is finite and irreplaceable.

Toni Sing Real Estate
At Rennie & Associates Realty

Greater Vancouver

Dynamic. Diligent. Enthusiastic.
Toni offers a high level of professional real estate service throughout Greater Vancouver. She currently resides at Rennie & Associates Realty in Vancouver, B.C. Her competitive advantage is that she treats clients uniquely by providing them with the knowledge to make informed decisions about their real estate investment. Toni has an excellent reputation with her clients and colleagues in the real estate industry.

Specialty: Real Estate Services
51 E Pender St, Vancouver, 604.808.3783
tonising.com, Twitter: @TSingRealEstate
facebook.com/ToniSingRealEstate
linkedin.com/in/ToniSingRealEstate

Photos by Kari Heese

Vals Fauquier and
Faye Fitzgerald

Q&A

What tip would you give women who are starting a business?
Be consistent with the quality of what you offer customers!

What do you like best about owning a business?
I get along better with the boss.

Who is your role model or mentor?
A woman, Kathleen Ringham, who taught me the value of image, perseverance, self-actualization and gratitude.

What is your motto or theme song?
Leonard Cohen's "If It Be Your Will." The song speaks of the power that exists beyond our human self and challenges us to find our authentic voice.

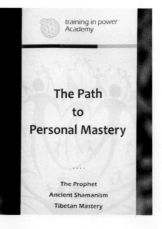

training in power
Academy

The Path to Personal Mastery

. . . .

The Prophet
Ancient Shamanism
Tibetan Mastery

Training in Power™ Academy

Vancouver, British Columbia

Enlightening. Transformative. Cutting-edge.
Training in Power™ Academy is a personal empowerment training system using unique metaphysical techniques to promote self-actualization, wellness and manifestation. You will find your balance through awareness of true power and destiny-driven spiritual advancement. Founded in 1986, and now in 20-plus North American cities, with headquarters in Vancouver, BC, and Seattle, WA.

Specialties: Empowerment Training, Energy Healing, Meditation
800.280.5753, traininginpower.com, facebook.com/TIPAcademy

Photos by Vairdy Photography

"The desire to be effective motivates us. To know that everyone has a destiny, and to help with that manifestation, is the passion and drive behind our work."

—Vals Fauquier and Faye Fitzgerald of
  Training in Power™ Academy

Unity Clothing Inc.

Lower Lonsdale, North Vancouver

Inviting. Diverse. Stylish.
A small boutique offering quality local and international brands that appeal to all ages. Unity boasts a one-stop shop where mom and daughter can find complete outfits to fit their personal style. Also offering urban menswear from denim to casual sweaters and locally designed underwear. Shop our unique accessories and comfortable footwear to complete any look!

Specialty: Fashion-forward Clothing
108 Victory Ship Way, North Vancouver, 604.988.8700
facebook.com/UnityClothing, Twitter: @Unityclothing_

Photos by Joanna Moss

Lori Simcox and Heidi George

Q&A

What tip would you give women who are starting a business?
Make sure you know your profit potential and all your costs. Ensuring that you account for all expenses before you start will help determine your success.

What do you like best about owning a business?
The ability to fulfill a dream and adapt it to the needs of our customers.

What motivates you on a daily basis?
We love seeing our customers come through the doors every day.

What do you CRAVE?
Continued success in the ever-evolving retail industry, and for Unity's brand to one day become a household name.

Vairdy Photography

Vancouver, British Columbia

Inspired. Natural. Candid.

Vairdy Andrew is an award-winning lifestyle portrait photographer specializing in maternity, babies, and families. With a photographic style that is classic, clean and candid, her calm energy allows her to really connect with her clients, creating honest and natural imagery. Each session with Vairdy Photography takes place at her clients' homes or at one of the many beautiful outdoor locations that the Lower Mainland has to offer.

Specialties: Love and New Beginnings, Baby and Family Portraits
778.668.7168, vairdy.com, facebook.com/vairdyphotography
Twitter: @vairdy, linkedin.com/in/vairdyandrew

Photos by Vairdy Photography

Vairdy Andrew

Q&A

What are your most popular products or services?
My most popular package is two sessions, Belly to Baby. Whether it's the magical first pregnancy or you've done it before, it's a great way to document these fleeting moments.

What tip would you give women who are starting a business?
Make sure you truly believe in what you do, it will shine through. Believe in yourself, be yourself and don't give up.

What do you like best about owning a business?
Freedom. Making my schedule and doing work I feel passionate about. I love holding myself accountable.

Doreen Tarampi

Q&A

What are your most popular products or services?
Ventura Financial helps growing companies create and execute successful financial strategies. Comprehensive tax preparation and business services include but are not limited to corporate taxes/ T2, bookkeeping, financial statement preparation and risk management.

What tip would you give women who are starting a business?
Outsource an accountant and create value in your company by keeping proper records of your financial data.

What do you like best about owning a business?
The infinite possibility of growth and creative independence.

Ventura Financial Strategies

Vancouver, British Columbia

Strategic. Accurate. Confidential.
As the president, you've succeeded in growing revenues, but this growth has brought unanticipated consequences. Your in-house bookkeeping system can't keep up. You're grateful for the growth, but you could do without the financial confusion. Ventura Financial Strategies provides clarity, control and continued growth through financial strategy, proven accounting processes and a new, clear view of your business.

Specialties: Financial Accounting, Taxation Services
604.818.8669, doreen@venturafinancial.ca
venturafinancial.ca, Twitter: @DoreenTarampi

Photos by Vairdy Photography

Amber George

Q&A

What are your most popular
products or services?
We are the only salon in North Vancouver
that carries the exclusive Shu Uemura Art
of Hair line. Our Art of Consultation is also
a favourite, regardless of the service.

What tip would you give women
who are starting a business?
Plan it well. Don't rush into it. Plan to
work long and hard: success takes
sacrifice. Do it for the love of doing
it, even when you aren't loving it.

What do you like best about
owning a business?
I like the visioning and strategizing,
and then putting the plans into
action and seeing the results. I love
watching the dream evolve into
fruition. I like the challenge of it.

Verve Hair Lounge

North Vancouver, British Columbia

Inspired. Gracious. Knowledgeable.
Verve Hair Lounge is an award-winning, eco-conscious Shu Uemura and Redken
boutique hair salon and art gallery. This warm and inviting salon houses some of the
country's best hair talent whose motto is: Hair Is Our Art, and You Are Our Inspiration.
Verve teammates bring a unique blend of talent, ambition and service, providing
hair and makeup services to loyal clients and the fashion/entertainment world.

Specialties: Hair and Makeup
227 Lonsdale Ave, North Vancouver, 778.340.4654
vervehairlounge.com
facebook.com/vervehairlounge, Twitter: @vervehair

Photos by Vairdy Photography

Photos by Kari Heese

Vibrational Fitness Training

Vancouver, British Columbia

Vital. Life-enhancing. Fun.
Vibrational Fitness Training is an innovative approach to fitness and wellness. Combining various physical disciplines (both Eastern and Western, ancient and modern) with meditation and specific breathing, the participant gains vitality, strength and agility quickly. Surprising to everyone: You do not have to attend in person to realize these achievements!

Anne Binning

Q&A

What do you like best about owning a business?
I love the freedom to be innovative. The opportunities that show up are extraordinary, and they present in a way I couldn't have even imagined. It's very exciting!

What motivates you on a daily basis?
I love my life. Helping people and watching them shift and grow into their health and wellness and turn those goals into a lifestyle.

What place inspires you?
Living on the West Coast in one of the most beautiful places on the planet. It truly is magical living here. Amazing people. Great dining experiences.

Specialties: Physical Workouts, Meditation, Healing
604.929.9535, annebinning.com

Wear Else

Kitsilano, Oakridge and West Vancouver

Effortless. Approachable. Savvy.
Wear Else features the best women's contemporary clothing, shoe and accessory brands all under one roof. Wear Else has complimentary personal shoppers that cater to every woman's need and budget, and their warm, friendly atmosphere makes this boutique chain one of the city's most approachable fashion destinations!

Specialty: Contemporary Women's Fashion
2360 West 4th Ave, Vancouver, 604.732.3521
Oakridge Mall: 650 West 41st Ave
Ste 119, Vancouver, 604.266.3613
Park Royal Mall, North Side, Second Level:
2015 Park Royal S, West Vancouver, 604.925.0058
wearelse.com, facebook.com/WearElseFashion
Twitter: @WearElse

Portrait by Joanna Moss

Zahra Mamdani

Q&A

What do you like best about owning a business?
The chance to help create something new and unique in the Vancouver marketplace. The chance to choose which causes we want to support and how. The chance to empower women.

What motivates you on a daily basis?
The women who shop in my stores. I am thrilled each time a customer finds the right shoe, dress or bag that makes them feel just that much more confident.

What place inspires you?
New York. I lived there for two years, and I am back there several times each year. There is just such an unbelievable energy and can-do attitude in that city!

Wear Those Deals

Vancouver, British Columbia

Stylish. Unique. Charitable.

Wear Those Deals delivers stylish deals to its fashion-loving subscribers. Committed to their community, Wear Those Deals cares deeply about the retailers they represent, and they're excited about their program "Wear Those Deals Gives Back."

Q&A

Sue Dickie

What are your most popular products or services?
Fashion deals from retailers in the Lower Mainland and online shops.

What tip would you give women who are starting a business?
Choose something you are passionate about. Don't give up. There will be bad days; learn from them! If you want a 9 to 5, Monday to Friday job, don't start a business!

What do you like best about owning a business?
Seeing other businesses succeed through their relationship with us!

What place inspires you?
Beautiful BC! Though I love to travel, I always look forward to coming home.

Let the
Fashionistas
Unite!!
Stylish deals starting at a
50% discount!!!
www.wearthosedeals.com

Specialties: Fashion Deals and Marketing
778.240.4961, wearthosedeals.com
facebook.com/wearthosedeals, Twitter: @wearthosedeals
pinterest.com/wearthosedeals, linkedin.com/in/suedickie

Rubina Mangat

Q&A

What tip would you give women who are starting a business?
Just do it! There is so much you can try to learn and prepare for beforehand, but truly, the learning begins only after you have taken the leap!

What do you like best about owning a business?
Being able to fully expand the creative/entrepreneurial energy that stirs within. You are in charge. It is very empowering, and overwhelming at times!

What motivates you on a daily basis?
Knowing that the only person who's getting in the way of me achieving what I want for that day, for that moment, is me. Each day is an opportunity.

Whisper
Photography & Jewels

Vancouver, British Columbia

Dreamy. Creative. Expressive.

Whisper Photography & Jewels came about when photography met metal! This distinctive line of jewels has put a unique spin on vintage designs. Each artisan jewel depicts a photograph from one of Rubina's adventures around the world. She takes you with her, as each piece comes with a personalized story. Custom design services are also available to clients.

Specialty: Unique Photographic Jewellery
whisperjewels.com, Twitter: @WhisperJewels

Photos by Kari Heese

Alisa Folk and
Kathie West Folk

Q&A

What are your most popular
products or services?
Our nail polish bar: butter London,
Deborah Lippmann, NCLA. Our panty
selection: Hanky Panky, Honeydew,
Björn Borg, Commando. Our beauty
products: Geisha Ink, Sara Happ,
Principessa, FarmHouse Fresh.

What tip would you give women
who are starting a business?
Find a partner who you can really trust.

What do you like best about
owning a business?
Making people happy just
by shopping for them!

What is your biggest fear?
If the world ran out of mascara!

wish.list boutique

Kitsilano, Vancouver

Stylish. Unique. Helpful.
wish.list is an LA-inspired specialty boutique stocked with the best of beauty, cosmetics, undies, nail polish, jewelry, handbags, girly gifts and more. With the variety of girly goods, it is impossible to leave wish.list without a gift for someone special or a gift for yourself!

Specialties: Beauty, Nail Polish, Cosmetics, Undies, Jewelry
2811 W Broadway, Vancouver, 604.676.8070
wishlistboutique.ca, facebook.com/wishlistboutiqueinc
Twitter: @wishlistboutiqu

Write Ahead

Gastown, Vancouver

Confident. Credible. Authentic.
Write Ahead produces dynamic business writing that's sprinkled with your personality and works for your business. Their team helps entrepreneurs create business plans that are concise, clear, thorough, well researched and injected with a little bit of passion. They develop unique copy that drives sales and attracts customers, and can make your writing shine, too.

Specialties: Business Plans, Copy Writing, Editing
119 W Pender, Ste 115, Vancouver
604.568.4227
writeahead.ca
facebook.com/writeahead
Twitter: @writeahead
linkedin.com/in/jessicaoman

Photos by Kari Heese

WRITE AHEAD
Business Writing and Consulting

Jessica Oman

Q&A

What are your most popular products or services?
We write a lot of business plans to help entrepreneurs get bank loans. Small-business owners needing less than $250K in start-up capital love our business plan packages.

What tip would you give women who are starting a business?
Don't try to do everything on your own—get help from experts who will get you to launch faster. And ask questions—entrepreneurs love to help each other.

What is your motto or theme song?
We can fix this! We make okay business ideas great, and turn poor writing into perfect prose.

"*Every day is completely different. I love experimenting with tactics and strategies for my business and then seeing what works. A business is a giant puzzle with infinite pieces!*"

—Jessica Oman of Write Ahead

Yapes Paints
Art by April Lacheur

White Rock, British Columbia

Bold. Inspiring. Whimsical.

April Lacheur is a self-taught acrylic painter who creates bold and unique pieces that bring life to any space. Trees with twisting trunks, bright florals and long-legged birds are her specialties. Her art cards and prints can be found in retail locations across Canada as well as at artisan markets and in her online store.

April Lacheur

Q&A

What are your most popular products or services?
I'm most well known for my paintings of trees with twisting trunks. My fun long-legged "lofty" birds and paintings that incorporate metal are becoming very popular.

What tip would you give women who are starting a business?
Be patient. Allow your business time to grow with you. There is a lot to learn along the way. Make sure to take the time to enjoy the process.

What do you like best about owning a business?
I get paid to paint! And some days, I can work from home in my pajamas.

Specialty: Acrylic Paintings
604.764.0295, YapesPaints.com
facebook.com/yapespaints, Twitter: @YapesPaints
linkedin.com/in/april-lacheur

"Live each day like its your last... and leave your heart on the canvas."

—April Lacheur of Yapes Paints

Zing Paperie & Design

North Shore, West Vancouver

Fresh. Unique. Chic.

Fine, fun and fabulous stationery is what you'll find at Zing Paperie & Design, a one-of-a-kind paper store located in the happening Village at Park Royal in West Vancouver. This bright and airy boutique is filled with stylish, earth-friendly note cards, modern invitations that you can personalize, beautiful wrappings, lovely gifts and many other goodies that are sure to inspire.

Specialties: Paper Goods, Gifts and Personalized Stationery
The Village at Park Royal: H1 - 925 Main St, West Vancouver
604.912.0246, zingdesign.ca
facebook.com/ZingPaperie, Twitter: @zingpaperie

Photos by Joanna Moss, except upper-left photo by cedar+gray

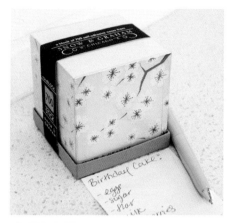

Tiffany Barkman

Q&A

What tip would you give women who are starting a business?
Love what you do. It will help you through the challenges of starting and running your business.

What do you like best about owning a business?
Besides the personal satisfaction and benefits of running a successful business, and being able to encourage and empower others on the journey... I appreciate the autonomy.

What place inspires you?
My favourite beach house getaway. Getting away is refreshing. Plus, I love this spot as a wonderful place to spend time with those dear to me.

Index by Category

by Category (continued)

Index by Location

by Location (continued)

Contributors

We believe in acknowledging, celebrating and passionately supporting locally owned businesses and entrepreneurs. We are extremely grateful to all contributors for this publication.

Melody Biringer, CRAVE Founder

thecravecompany.com, startupjunkie.com

Innovative. Feminine. Connective.
Melody Biringer, self-avowed "start-up junkie," has built companies that range from Biringer Farm, a family-run specialty-food business, to home furnishings to a fitness studio.

Her current entrepreneurial love-child is The CRAVE Company: designed to creatively connect entrepreneurs who approach business in a fresh new way with the consumers they desire, as well as with each other. CRAVE is a resource for women entrepreneurs to promote their business and support like-minded women, and CRAVEguides are your go-to source for anything you could ever wish to find in your city—exclusively from women. Melody has taken CRAVE from Seattle to more than 30 cities worldwide, including New York City, Boston, Los Angeles, Chicago, Amsterdam and Toronto. Melody is a loyal community supporter, versed traveler and strong advocate for women-owned businesses.

What are your most popular products or services?
The global CRAVE community connects savvy business owners through online networks and in-person events. We believe in the power of collaboration among smart, successful women entrepreneurs, and we facilitate these relationships through our dynamic community. Our new online directory creates a hub for discovering women-owned businesses, with personal insights to attract followers to your business and encourage them to pursue dreams of their own.

What was the motivation behind starting your business?
I saw my best friend twice in a year and thought, "This is not right." So I created excuses to get together so that we'd get it on the calendar, instead of giving it lip service. I crave girlfriend time.

What is your motto or theme song?
"Flashdance... What a Feeling" by Irene Cara. "What a feeling... Take your passion and make it happen... I can have it all; now I'm dancing for my life..." Every time I'm feeling a bit low, I play that song, and my spirits lift immediately.

Ronak Samadi
CRAVE Vancouver Partner

Twitter: @ronaksamadi, linkedin.com/in/rsamadi

Dynamic. Ambitious. Inspired.
Ronak is a senior at the University of British Columbia and has been a partner of CRAVE Vancouver for over two years. As one of CRAVE's youngest employees, Ronak combines her passions for community growth and women in business while meeting and supporting the eminent entreprenesses of the city.

With a passion for lifelong learning, she finds inspiration through meeting people from all walks of life as well as from traveling and the fine arts. The philosophy behind her work is limitless creativity, organization, determination and, most importantly, a positive attitude. This aspiring entrepreness looks forward to all her enriching future endeavours.

Christa Leigh Meister
CRAVE Vancouver Partner

christa@stylebybusiness.com
Twitter: @stylebybusiness

Charming. Genuine. Reliable.
Christa has been an entrepreneur and a freelance consultant for the last five years and has worked for companies throughout Canada and the United States. Her work has included production and business development as well as strategic planning, and now it's expanded to image consulting. Christa deliberately works from the inside out, consciously employing both traditional and innovative techniques.

Christa's passion is assisting women in all areas of development, and she believes in building solid long-term partnerships that effectively enrich the lives of those involved.

Alison Turner, Graphic Designer

alisonjturner.com, linkedin.com/in/alisont

Alison is a passionate designer and critical thinker from Seattle. She supports human rights and the local food movement. She enjoys researching interesting things, volunteering, being outside, dancing, cooking and running.

Amanda Buzard, Lead Designer

amandabuzard.com

Amanda is a graphic designer, aspiring DIYer and former Seattleite who recently relocated to San Francisco. She's inspired by clean patterns and textiles, and has a thirst for learning, tinkering and exploring. In her spare time she enjoys taking pictures, baking pies and going on adventures.

Carrie Wicks, Copy Editor

linkedin.com/in/carriewicks

Carrie has been proofreading professionally for 14-plus years in mostly creative fields. When she's not proofreading/copyediting, she's reading, singing jazz, walking in the woods or gardening.

Sarah Granger, Research Intern

Twitter: @sarahhnoelle

Sarah is an ambitious lover of all things fashion. She is working toward a business marketing degree and actively interns with various public relations firms in Vancouver and New York.

Jennifer Williams, Photographer

jenniferwilliams.com, facebook.com/JenniferWilliamsBoudoirStudio,
Twitter: @boudoir_studio

Jennifer Williams is a Vancouver-based boudoir photographer whose
beautiful use of light and natural retouching ensure timeless images that
can be enjoyed for years to come.

Joanna Moss, Photographer

joannamoss.com, photography@joannamoss.com
Twitter: @Joanna__Moss, 604.613.9474

Joanna Moss specializes in natural light, on-location photography.
Focusing on lifestyle portraits and weddings, she creates unforgettable,
personalized pieces of art that can be treasured for generations. Joanna
works throughout the Greater Vancouver area, Squamish and Whistler.

Kari Heese, Photographer

boutiquestudios.ca, Twitter: @boutiquestudios, 604.558.4848

Kari is an award-winning photographer who has traveled the world
photographing weddings. She has perfected an organic and creative
approach that keeps her images fresh yet classic and timeless.

Karolina Turek Photography

karolinaturek.com, Twitter: @karolinaturek

From shooting international celebrities to Vancouver locals, Karolina's
style stands out among the rest. Her key to successful headshots is
creating a fun, easygoing and comfortable atmosphere.

Vairdy Photography, Photographer

vairdy.com, facebook.com/vairdyphotography, Twitter: @vairdy

Vairdy Andrew is an award-winning lifestyle portrait photographer specializing in maternity, babies, and families. Her style is classic, clean and candid. Her calm energy allows her to connect with clients and create honest and natural imagery.

Get the savings you crave with the following participating businesses—one time only!

Acupoint Wellness Centre
$20 off a consultation and acupuncture or biopuncture treatment (first-time clients only)

Baobei Lashes & Company
free shipping or delivery in Vancouver

The Bar Method
10% discount

Because You Said So
10% discount

bloom
free lubricant with the purchase of Bloom Essentials

body politic
20% discount (regular-priced items only)

Boutique Studios
10% off a portrait session

Busy Bump Maternity Services
20% discount

Changes Clothing & Jewellery Bar
40% off two or more consigned clothing items

Cutie Pie Wax Bar
10% discount

Della Optique Optometry & Eyewear
20% discount on frames

Design Project
15% discount

Favourite Gifts
15% discount

Filou Designs
10% discount

Forum for Women Entrepreneurs (FWE)
$20 off a 1-year membership

Hagensborg Chocolates Ltd.
15% discount

Hear at Home Mobile Hearing Clinic LTD
10% off custom-made swim plugs, sleeper plugs, musician molds or ear defenders (in store and by appointment only)

It's Your Move
10% discount ($100 minimum order, not applicable with other offers)

Jennifer Williams Boudoir Photography
25% off album purchases

Karolina Turek Photography
$100 off any photography package

Le Petit Spa
20% off a service

- [ ] Lé Soirées Weddings & Events
  15% discount

- [ ] Lotus Destiny
  20% discount

- [ ] mom inc MOVEMENT
  25% off 3 month BOSS listing

- [ ] Opus Talis Designs
  50% off colour logo, with full branding package

- [ ] PEARL Teeth Whitening Spa
  25% off any service

- [ ] Porchlight Press
  15% off your first letterpress printing order

- [ ] Salon M2 Hair and Skin
  20% off any hair service

- [ ] Saucisse Restaurant
  free appetizer with purchase of entree

- [ ] Shine Nail Bar
  15% discount

- [ ] SKN Holistic Rejuvenation Clinic
  25% discount

- [ ] Steveston Village Maternity
  15% discount

- [ ] Sweet Dreams & Flying Machines
  10% discount

- [ ] Training in Power Academy
  $100 off a course (in teaching locations only)

- [ ] Unity Clothing Inc.
  10% discount

- [ ] Vairdy Photography
  10% discount

- [ ] Verve Hair Lounge
  20% discount

- [ ] Vibrational Fitness Training
  20% discount

- [ ] Wear Else
  15% discount

- [ ] Whisper Photography & Jewels
  30% off an artisan piece or 50% off a custom piece

- [ ] wish.list boutique
  20% discount

- [ ] Yapes Paints - Art by April Lacheur
  25% discount

- [ ] Zing Paperie & Design
  15% discount (excludes design services)

Use code CRAVE for online discount when applicable.

Details of discounts may vary from business to business, so please call first.
The CRAVE company shall not be held responsible for variations on discounts at individual businesses. This page may not be photocopied or otherwise duplicated.